Congratulations Robert

MW01254665

Molé Mama

A Memoir

of

Love, Cooking and

Loss

Diana M. Silva

Remember our love is the key to all.
Wishing you the very best!

Diana Silva

For
Rose Ybarra Silva

My heart will always long to hear your voice, hold your hand and cook with you!

Contents

Foreword

I didn't know how long I had to say goodbye, but I can tell you the precise moment I understood my mother and I were beginning our goodbyes. Christmas morning 2012, my sister was calling me but when I spoke into the phone, she wasn't speaking. When she did summon words, her voice trembled. Our mother had suffered a massive stroke.

The year I met the lovely Diana Silva, we were both mourning our mothers and reconstructing our shattered hearts. We each held a glimmer of light that somehow, the loss of our mothers was the cracking open of a new life, a life that needed to be different – more generous, more loving, more meaningful.

When you lose a great love, you feel a bottomless void. You hold a dissonance in your mind, the feeling that the person occupied an immense space in your heart, mind and soul and yet the unfathomable thought that the person is simply not here.

When a daughter loses a mother, she loses, for a little while, a sense of her place in the world.

When I met Diana, all she knew was a place she could begin: She had a story ready to be shared – a story of love.

That story not only needed to be told, it needed to be lived. This was our synchronicity, that we each had this idea about our lives at the same time – a new story to be lived. This idea brought solace. It brought purpose. It brought us together as author and editor. And it brought a rebirth.

Diana and I often say we are like sisters, though we have never met in person. I believe that is so because we each had mothers who lived true to their values – love, family, connection, generosity, nurturing, gentleness, beauty, forgiveness, wisdom. Her mother was named Rose and shared her heart through food. My mother loved roses and shared her heart through music.

It feels like Diana and I are sisters because we knew the same kind of love, a fiercely loyal and generous kind of love that draws more and more loving people into the fold. As you'll discover in the story you're about to read, what defines the family of Rose Ybarra Silva is that it just sort of brims over. In

Diana's mother's heart, and from her mother's stove, there was always plenty.

When her journey began, Diana was at a loss as to how she could say goodbye to her dear sweet mama. She didn't believe it was possible. So she did what her mother had taught her. Show up at the stove. Cook with love. Give with all your heart.

This story leads you through an extraordinary goodbye. I urge you to read it with a courageous heart, for that is the way Diana has lived it and written it. We want to look away from grief. We don't know what to do. In this story, Diana shows up for the grief. And she keeps showing up. My hope is that she also has shown us how we can show up for goodbye.

I have told you the sad part now. But the truth is, grief is a two-sided coin. We can find great joy in remembering a life well-lived and treasuring the gifts of that life to us. The life of Rose Ybarra Silva was not one that often gets told, not the stuff of movie blockbusters. Yet the heroines of our lives are the ones who make a difference with their love.

In this book, Diana invites you to let yourself feel the beautiful sadness of losing someone. There is indeed an exquisite aspect of loss– and a funny part, a tender part, a magical part – and Diana has captured those here.

In these scenes of Diana at her mother's side, sharing as her mother taste-tests Diana's renditions of her mother's heirloom recipes, Diana has given us something else as well. She has given us a portrait of the handing down of love, wisdom and tradition. She has given us a picture of reverence for a life of meaning.

Carolyn Flynn
Albuquerque, NM

Introduction

I must have been about nine or ten when I first held the *tejolote* in my small hands, cooking with my mother in her kitchen as she taught me how to grind garlic in our magical *molcajete* (mol-cah-hay'-tay). I loved how loud and fun it was to pound into the stone bowl. I thought that everyone had one, and it's what made my mother's recipes impossible to duplicate and so delicious. My mother used it all the time to grind spices and garlic and it sat proudly on her kitchen counter.

The molcajete you see on my book cover is that magical tool, made of basalt rock, and it belonged to my Mexican grandmother Magdalena. It is over 100 years old. Grandma Magdalena was 40 years old when she left Mexico with her magical molcajete and crossed the border into this country illegally in the early 1920s.

I can picture her, just five feet tall, olive-skinned, her dark hair in a single long braid, with this molcajete packed in her only suitcase as she walked across.

Grandma Magdalena settled in Betteravia, California, with her family. She and her six children worked in the fields, tending and harvesting vegetables. In 1927, she gave birth to her youngest daughter, Rose – my mother.

About ten years later she was running a boarding house that was home to male migrant farm workers, and my grandmother and my mother cooked three meals for them daily. Menus included complex mole sauces, tacos, Spanish rice, chorizo and papas, chile rellenos, refried beans, Mexican soups, salsas and so much more. And every meal included warm, fluffy homemade flour tortillas.

Though I was born just a few months after she died, I know the stories of Grandma Magdalena's magical cooking and her life from the stories my mother told me. Grandma Magdalena's magical molcajete was always with her and used to crush spices and garlic for concocting her spicy delicious recipes.

Grandma Magdalena was a very spiritual woman, her house filled with saints and burning candles. Anytime death was near for a loved one, villagers summoned Grandma Magdalena, who would immediately rush to the side of the dying. Grandma Magdalena would pray, hold their hands and stay with them as they took their last breaths.

I decided to photograph the molcajete on wood to highlight my mother's family's humble beginnings in central Mexico. They lived in an adobe house with dirt floors in San Nicolas de Ibarra.

Grandma Magdalena's courage, grace and compassion for the dying inspired me to find the courage to support my mother during her final 13 months. I knew it was going to be the hardest thing I'd ever done in my entire life, to witness my best friend die.

And this is the story of my heartfelt goodbye to my mother, Rose Ybarra Silva, inspired by another remarkable woman, Grandma Magdalena, whom I never met.

Diana Magdalene Silva

Chapter One

Three Days to Say Goodbye

A doctor, a family member or friend utters
those dreaded words:

*"There's nothing more that can be done but to
make your loved one comfortable."*

This final prognosis may leave you numb,

bewildered, distraught, sad and helpless.

It's really happening and there's nothing

left to do but be present with your loved one.

Tuesday, Dec. 6, 2010

Silicon Valley's Highway 101 South morning commute was slow, and my mind wandered to planning the menu for our weekend barbecue. I still hadn't mastered my mother's legendary chili beans. Was the magic ingredient cumin or cloves? None of her recipes had ever been written down, but I knew I needed to do so soon. I'd call her on my evening commute and ask her again which one it was.

Mom's chili beans were a cherished staple at all our large Mexican family celebrations. She helped me make them for the baptism of my oldest son, Gabriel, 14 years ago. Mom had come to visit a few days before the big party to help me cook. She walked me through every step of her chili bean recipe: rehydrating the dried pinto beans by simmering them on the stove for several hours; frying the hamburger, bacon, and chorizo (spicy Mexican sausage); and removing the extra fat. Then we crushed the peeled garlic cloves in my grandmother's magical molcajete, adding in chopped onions, dried California chile powder, salt, pepper and … either cumin and cloves.

That part I couldn't summon from my memory. We tasted tested the chili beans and added more spices until Mom gave them her master chef stamp of approval and we lowered the heat so the beans could simmer for a couple of hours.

I left the kitchen for a few minutes to fill Gabriel's giant Dalmatian piñata with candy and place bright floral arrangements throughout the house. Mom and I had hung streamers and balloons earlier. The yummy aromas from Mom's Spanish rice, chili beans, salsas and grilled meats wafted through the house, making it feel welcoming and festive.

When I returned to the kitchen, I took a long look at my beautiful Mama holding baby Gabriel as she stirred the chili beans. Over her longish black dress with little pink flowers, she wore my homemade 49er apron. Her short curly strawberry blond hair was neatly combed, and her warm round face beamed with pride and joy. At 70, my mother, Rose Ybarra Silva, had already lived much longer than she had ever expected. Gabriel was 5 months, and already he'd stolen his grandmother's heart with his dark curly hair, big brown eyes, bright smile and love of her yummy food.

"He wanted to see his beans," Mom said as she slowly stirred and Gabriel peered into the big pot.

"He's already a foodie," I said, moving in to kiss his forehead. "What did you do to the beans?"

"They weren't spicy enough," Mom said with a little grin.

"You always wait until I leave the kitchen and then you rework them. I can tell because they're a darker color of red now," I said.

"They taste better, too," Mom said with a big smile.

"Oh Mom, I need you to teach me every secret, and I won't learn if you keep fixing my recipes," I said.

"You're already a great cook, Mia," she said.

"But I want to be as good as you someday." I hugged her and thanked her.

After the baptismal ceremony, our guests joyfully filled their plates with rice, chili beans, potato salad, carne asada, grilled chicken, roasted garlic bread, guacamole, linguica and Mom's homemade flour tortillas. As always, newbies to my mom's recipes had the same comments for her, "This is the best Mexican food I've ever eaten."

That's the day she gave me my most cherished possession. After all our guests had gone home and we were doing the dishes, she began. "Diana, I want you to have your Grandma Magdalena's magical molcajete," she said as she fondly held the black three-legged mortar and pestle in both hands. "As you know she carried this in her one and only suitcase as she illegally immigrated from Mexico. Now that Daddy is gone, I wanted to make sure I gave it to you, just in case something happens to me," Mom said tenderly.

"But you still use it, Mom. You're not going anywhere for a long time." Tears filled my eyes. "You can give it to me later."

"I have lots of other molcajetes, Diana," she said. "I want you to have it and I'm sure your grandma agrees. You love to cook and I know you will continue to use it."

"Mom, you're right. I will always use her magical molcajete. And now that it belongs to me, maybe its magic will finally make my food as good as yours."

When I hugged her tight, it was with a full understanding that my beautiful mom had just given me her family inheritance.

***

Highway 101 South deposited me at my work, so I parked my car and went into the office just like any other day. So how did I know, at 10 o'clock, sitting in a meeting room in Silicon Valley, 239 miles from my mother in Santa Maria on California's Central Coast, surrounded at a table by 15 other colleagues that I should call her? I had sat for about 30 minutes with an all-too-familiar feeling. Something was wrong. I needed to call. At last, the meeting ended – what the big takeaways were, I could never tell you – and I was sprung loose. I frantically dialed, not my mother's number but an emergency room in Santa Maria, four hours away down Highway 101.

"Marian Medical Center, emergency room, how can I help you?" answered a woman with a cheerful voice.

"Is my mother, Rose Silva, one of your recent patient arrivals?" I asked nervously. "I live in the Bay area and I think she's just arrived."

"Yes, she's here," the woman said, and I struggled to stay calm.

I took a deep breath as I heard the cheerful woman's voice come through my phone. "She's being evaluated," she said. "Your sister is with her."

I ended the call and I felt anxious and sad. My poor mama was in the hospital again – fourth time this year.

* * *

Should I stay or should I go? My heart wanted to race out of work and head down the coast to her. But my dear sweet mother had been battling congestive heart disease and chronic obstructive pulmonary disease (COPD) for the past five years and she'd become a hospital regular.

No point in calling my youngest sister Isabella for at least 30 minutes. I knew the emergency room drill, but it didn't make the waiting any easier. My heart was racing and my breath was shallow as various scenarios of Mom's complicated health raced through my mind. I needed to calm down. I said a prayer at my desk and tried to return a few emails, but it was impossible to stop thinking about Mom. I kept seeing her large brown eyes, so frightened, and I longed to hold her hand while the doctor evaluated her breathing and her heart. My co-workers talked quietly in surrounding cubicles, but I only wanted to hear one voice. Hers. I wanted to hear, "I'm OK, Mia."

Mia is Spanish for mine, and she had used this term of endearment with me all of my life. Every time I heard her say it, I simply felt loved. I knew it meant I belonged to her.

Mom had stopped driving the previous year and used oxygen permanently now. She was 83 and lived alone with her two Yorkshire terriers, Lulu and Gigi.

She had refused countless invitations to move in with Isabella or me because she wanted to maintain her independence and didn't want to burden us.

But she still cooked.

Rose was the reigning "best cook" in our large Mexican family of about 300 people when you counted all the *tias*, *tios* and cousins. She'd learned to cook from our family master, my grandmother, book

Magdalena. For ten years, Rose had helped Magdalena run a small boarding house for migrant farmworkers in Betteravia, just a few miles west of Santa Maria, and that's where she'd mastered the art of seriously delicious Mexican food.

My sons, 14-year-old Gabriel and 11-year-old Jessie, adored their Grandma Rose and loved her cooking. Our visits to her house always began with the same tradition. We'd exchange kisses and hugs at her front door and then we'd go to her kitchen. We knew to arrive hungry. The short walk to the kitchen was a culinary treasure of Mexican food aromas and reminded me that I was truly home. The boys would sit on their stools at the counter directly in front of her brown stove. She would immediately start making them her legendary flour tortillas. Sometimes she served them with butter and other times she made them burritos. And she always made them Spanish rice, or as they called it her orange rice. I loved watching the boys joyfully eat their grandmother's delicious food and talk about school and sports. For the past five years she'd done this with her long oxygen cord, skillfully keeping it away from the stove and never complaining about her poor health.

And when it was time for us to go home, she had a sweet farewell tradition, too. Before she kissed Gabriel and Jessie goodbye she would give each of them a lunch bag with homemade burritos, chips and a yummy dessert. She said hello and goodbye to us with scrumptious tortillas.

* * *

Thirty frantic minutes. No call from Isabella. So I called her.

"The doctor thinks she has pneumonia again," Isabella said. "And she's having difficulty breathing. They're admitting her to the hospital."

I'd heard this diagnosis so many times before. Poor Mama, how I longed for her to be healthy, but I knew that wasn't the direction she was going.

I almost didn't hear Isabella say the doctor was waiting on lab results. The next thing I heard was, "How did you know that she was here again?" I chose not to respond to my sister's question. All that mattered right now was Mom's condition.

"I didn't call you, because I didn't want to

bother you at work," Isabella said.

"It's never a problem to call me about Mom," I said, and rushed ahead to the next question. "So do you think I need to come down to see her?"

"Not yet," came Isabella's answer, and in her tone I heard the stern registered nurse, all about lab tests and oxygen levels. This was her way of dealing with what we were both wondering: if this was the beginning of goodbye. "I'll let you know if anything changes, but she's stable right now. You should be able to talk to her later today after they get her settled in her room."

Now it was wait-and-see. Mom had been in and out of the hospital more than 20 times over the past five years. It was hard to know when to drop everything and make the four-hour drive to Santa Maria. I rehearsed a conversation in my head with my boss, who had been supportive. But I knew that at the end of the day, the bottom line was my performance, and although I'd always hit my goals in the past, I knew my real value was based only on how well we did every three months. Would I make my numbers for the quarter? I was the primary breadwinner for my family. My heart was torn. So many times my heart had been torn. There's what you have to do to support your family financially, and there's what your heart longs to do. What my heart wanted was to be with my mother.

***

Our daily conversations were a ritual. During the week I would call my mother, during my commute home. I'd go on and on about work, about my sons, about politics … anything and everything that was on my mind. She would listen. And I would feel soothed by her sweet voice. We'd been speaking for about 20 minutes every day since I got my first "real job" after college. We had our ritual down. On the weekends, I worked our calls around her sacred no-call time zones, such as Giants, Lakers or 49ers games or evening telenovelas.

I knew she would insist that I didn't need to come see her because she worried about me missing work and what it might mean to my employment status. My parents had a serious work ethic, and being a good employee and staying employed was of critical importance. I'd never lost a job, but Mom still worried about it.

Afterward, Isabella and I spoke for a few moments. Mom's pneumonia was being treated with intravenous antibiotics, and she'd be in the hospital for a couple of days. Isabella promised to let me know if her conditioned worsened. The whole time I listened to the medical facts Isabella shared, I struggled. I wondered if I could trust my sister's judgment. Sometimes I thought Isabella was in denial about my mother's failing health.

Thursday, Dec. 9, 2010

Three days with my mother in the hospital, and it was a big day for me. I was making my first presentation about our new website to hundreds of employees, and it was being videotaped so employees in our global offices could watch it, too. I hoped to get a copy soon so I could show it to Mom. She loved hearing about my job, my travels, and so on.

I spent the morning rehearsing. My presentation went well and ran for about two hours.

Then, it was back my desk to check my phone. I had several missed calls from my sister and an urgent voice mail.

"What's up, Sis?" I said as Isabella answered the phone.

"Why did you take so long to call us back?" she said. "I've been trying to reach you for hours."

I explained about the presentation. "I forgot my phone at my desk."

"Mom's not doing well, Diana," Isabella said.

Her words landed into my heart like giant blocks of concrete. Isabella went on, but I wasn't prepared for this turn of events.

"Her oxygen levels are really low, and her carbon dioxide levels are really high. Her doctor is concerned that she may go into a coma," Isabella said. "I think you need to come as soon as you can."

I was filled with regret for not heading out sooner. Why hadn't I listened to my intuition? I took a moment to compose myself. I called my boss and told him that I needed to leave work immediately. "I don't know when I'll be back," I said, and promised to update him as soon as I knew more. I gathered my team and said, "My mother's health is worse and I need to go see her. It was a struggle to hold back my tears. I looked into their horrified faces. They reassured me they would handle everything and not to worry about work.

I called my boyfriend, John, and my sons' John would pick up Gabriel l. At home, I packed our ell-trained trauma unit leader s all up. I knew exactly what all made these urgent trips thankfully, each time, Mom

s going to be okay?" Gabriel d the car.

"I'm not sure, Gabriel. I'm sure that she's scared, and it will help her to see all of us," I said.

"You worry too much, Mom. She'll be okay," Gabriel said.

I knew his response was more about him than me. He was really close to his grandma, and I don't think he could bear the thought of losing her.

At 2 p.m., I checked in with Isabella to let her

know we were on our way.

Arriving in Santa Maria about 3½ hours later, I said. "John, I need to see her alone for a few minutes. Can you stay with the boys in the waiting room?

"Whatever you need, honey," John said and offered to walk our little gray and white, shih tzu, Sophia. "We'll be in the waiting room. You just come get us when you're ready."

I kissed him on the cheek and started my solo walk into the hospital. My heart was racing, and I was trying to remain calm.

I knew that no matter how horrible Mom looked, I had to hold back the tears and be cheerful for her.

Isabella greeted me at the hospital door with a hug. "She's not doing well," she said. "Her breathing and oxygen levels aren't improving."

All I could think was: my sweet mama.

Entering her room, I went to the sink to wash my hands. "Hi, Mom," I said loudly so she could hear me. I was sure she didn't have her hearing aids in. She turned her head toward the sink across the room and gently smiled. "Ay, Diana, you were just here a few weeks ago, you shouldn't have come," her familiar I-don't-want-to-be-a-bother-voice.

I gave her a hug and held her hand. She was very pale. She tried to speak and coughed. She was wearing a hospital gown and her gray, thick wavy hair was showing signs of serious bed-head after four days in the hospital. Strands stood up on the back of her pillow.

I launched into cheerful chitchat as I told her about our drive down, traffic conditions on the 101, the boys' school activities, sports, Gabriel's Christmas concert and my job. She listened carefully, and this calmed her and allowed me to distract her from noticing how scared I was.

About ten minutes later, the boys arrived to give her hugs and chat a little. I scanned their faces, which showed their worry about their grandma. Gabriel managed to converse with her more about his recent concert. Jessie said very little and was visibly uncomfortable seeing his grandma so sick again. He suffered from asthma, and I wondered if he identified more with Mom's coughing attacks and her inability to breathe.

Visiting hours were over just a few minutes later, so John took the boys to Isabella's house for the night. Isabella went home, too, and I offered to spend the night at the hospital with my mama. She put up a little fuss about not wanting me to sleep in a chair and how I needed to rest, but this was our normal routine. If I was in Santa Maria and she was in the hospital, I stayed with her. I'd spent so many nights next to my mother's hospital bed in the past few years and I knew she was secretly delighted not to be alone.

Hospital stay — first night

Shortly after I arrived for the evening, Mom had a terrible coughing attack. I held her hand and rubbed her back as she coughed uncontrollably and gasped for air.

"Oh, Mia, it's so scary," she said. "This reminds me of when I had TB."

It was becoming more and more common for her to reference TB, and my attempts to learn more about this painful part of her life had failed in the past. She didn't like to speak about it. I knew that she had been removed from her family's home and placed in the Santa Barbara tuberculosis sanitarium when she was young. "How old were you when you were diagnosed with TB?"

"I was 17, it was 1943 and I was there for seven years. I think I got it from my aunt. She had been really sick and my mother had sent me to take care of her. Back then, no one knew what it was," she said. "I was one of the lucky ones."

I knew that she was referring to all of her relatives that had died in the sanitarium. Her older sister, brother-in-law, nephew and so many other cousins had lost their battles with TB. Seven years, though. It had been seven years of her life.

"I survived because of your cousin Maria," Mom said. "She was only seven when she joined me, and her father and brother both died while we were there. I was older, and I knew that I had to take care of her. Our families could only visit us once a year because it was so contagious. We had to lie on our backs all day and night. We could only bathe once a week. They gave us countless experimental drugs and treatments. Eventually they gave me surgery to remove two of my lung lobes. That's what saved my life."

I ventured more. "After surgery and the staying in bed for years, were you able to walk?"

"No. I had to learn to walk again when I was finally better." She abruptly got quiet.

My mother was a survivor. She knew difficult breathing. She had known it for almost 70 years.

I helped Mom brush her teeth and wash her face. I rubbed her arms and legs with lotion. The hospital noises made it hard for her to rest. Her nurse came in and gave her more meds, including a sleeping pill, and eventually she fell asleep. I sat in the chair next to her bed, holding her hand. She was struggling to breathe and looked frail and in pain. The essence of her being and positive outlook hid these things from the world in her waking hours because she was such a vibrant sweet soul. It was only when she was sleeping did I really witness the severity of her advancing diseases.

The day was coming when her suffering would be over. I tried to imagine my life without her. Oh, how was I going to live without her? The thought terrified me.

Why do we have to grow old? Why must our

health deteriorate? I wished to go back to the days when Mom could breathe.

I sat in the large blue reclining chair next to Mom's hospital bed and settled in for the night. One of the nurses brought me a blanket, and I texted with John and the boys for a little while and said my goodnights. I updated Isabella with the news that Mom was sleeping. John encouraged me to sleep, too. "Try to get some rest," he texted.

I had been sleeping for about three hours when I heard her screams. I jumped out of my chair. "Mom, what's wrong?" I asked looking at her confused face and flying arms. She didn't answer and continued to swing her arms about as she cried and screamed. I reached down and tried to caress her arms. I was afraid that she was going to accidentally pull out her IV. "Mom, it's me Diana. You're in the hospital," I said loudly as I tried to constrain her and stare into her eyes. Again no response, and the crying continued.

"She can't hear you, dear," the nurse said as she walked in and saw my panic. "Her carbon dioxide levels are too high."

"Is there anything we can do for her?" I asked.

"Hopefully it's just an episode and she'll be okay soon," the nurse replied and left us.

I tried hugging Mom, holding her hand, rubbing her forehead, but I couldn't soothe her. As her tears spilled, she spoke about my younger brother, who had been born dead, her red wagon that got broken when she was a little girl and her older brother dying. Then she spoke about my father's death, Joseph and how much she missed him. He had been dead for 16 years. I had never seen her this tormented, and it was crushing me. I lost my ability to hold back my tears, and they rolled down my cheeks as I stood by and helplessly watched her relive her greatest sorrows.

Eventually the crying ended and she calmed down. But she remained unresponsive to my efforts to communicate with her. Her spirit was rocked and full of sorrow.

* * *

Hours went by, and she remained unresponsive. I couldn't help my sweet mama, but perhaps our parish priest could. At 8 a.m., I called our church, but their number kept ringing busy, and I was sure that the number listed on their website was wrong. I needed a phone book, but couldn't leave Mom alone.

Isabella arrived a few hours later, and instructed me to go home immediately and get some rest. "I'm going to the lobby to find a phone book, Sis, and call the church," I said over my sister's protests. "Please stay with her. I'll be right back."

The nice lobby volunteer had just given me the phone book when Father George, my former high school principal, walked into the hospital.

"Father George, I was just trying to find your phone number. My mother, Rose Silva is here, and she is really ill."

I'm not sure he recognized me but he remembered Rose. My mother had made them yummy food for years and been a longtime parishioner.

"I'm here to see another patient," he said. "But I will come with you to see your mom first."

Mom was happy to see Father George and he gave her the anointing of the sick and Holy

Communion. She remained calm after Father George's visit, and I went to Isabella's house to sleep for a few hours.

Hospital stay — second night

I arrived to stay with Mom through the night. As I entered her room, the number of her visitors shocked me. Clearly her nurse was ignoring the hospital's visitation policies. There were more than 20 people standing around her hospital bed, including my sons and four other grandchildren. My oldest niece, Renee, had helped all my mother's grandchildren make cards and write letters. It was endearing to see them giving these to her when I entered her hospital room. Mom was so happy, and the kids were so proud of their presents. Mom tried to speak to them a little, but her coughing didn't allow her to say much.

The children all went home and I got a quick update from Isabella on my mother's medical condition. There had been no improvement in her oxygen or carbon dioxide levels, but she was clearly back to her sweet loving self.

I woke at about 1:30 a.m. to loud coughing and choking. The room was dark, and Mom was still sleeping. I got up and peered behind the curtain. Mom's roommate vomited uncontrollably. I ran to the nursing station for help, and two nurses raced in.

By 2 a.m. the commotion was over and the nurses had left the room. Mom's roommate seemed to be okay. All the lights were on, and I pulled back the curtain back to my mother's section of the room. I gasped as I saw her face.

Her lips were blue.

Once again, I ran to the nursing station. They called for backup, and in an instant, the room was full of nurses and doctors all trying to work on my sweet mama. I stood slightly outside the room, listening to all the noise. Machines wheeled past me as the effort mounted to save her. My heart raced, and my eyes filled with tears.

I stared at my phone and searched for my sister's number, or maybe I should call John's. I stopped. I would wait until I knew something, anything.

"She's unconscious," the young,

compassionate female doctor said. "Her oxygen levels are well below normal. We will do what we can, but we must move her to intensive care immediately."

They weren't sure if she'd slipped into a coma or had had a stroke. "We don't know," the doctor said. "But we will continue to try and save her."

The rest of the medical prognosis was a stream of long words. My brain translated: Mom might never wake up again.

"She's a Do Not Resuscitate (DNR) patient," the doctor continued. "So you understand that if your mother's heart stops, we will not restart it."

I confirmed that I understood. Yes, those were my mother's wishes.

***

Five hours later, Mom's doctor gathered us in the lobby. By this time, those assembled were John, Isabella, our brother Augustine and our sister Lena.

"I'm surprised that she's still with us," the doctor said. "We will know more in the next 24 hours."

She shared lots of details about Mom's night. "This was a perfect storm of tragic health events," she said. Mom was still unconscious, but the doctor thought we could visit her soon.

Isabella asked lots of questions as I looked around at my family. Most of us had a combination of tears in our eyes and terror on our faces. John hugged me.

After the doctor had left, a dead silence took hold in the room. The doctor's words echoed in my mind. "We were very fortunate to save her. She's a fighter."

A few minutes later, we were given the go-ahead to visit her, two at a time. John accompanied me when it was my turn. Mom was wearing a giant white Darth Vader breathing mask that covered most of her face. My sister had explained that the mask removed the excess carbon dioxide from her system. A gazillion other tubes connected to her. Despite all the medical wizardry around her, she looked peaceful as she slept. I held her hand for a few minutes as I fought back the tears. "I love you, Mom, you've been the best mama ever," I whispered in her ear and quietly left the room.

Hospital stay — third night

A few hours of sleep, and it was back to the hospital. To my delight, Mom was awake. She was frail and weak and oh so tired. Isabella had spent most of the day with her, and I would be spending the night with her again. Various family members had been by throughout the day as word made its way through Santa Maria about Mom's latest hospital visit.

Her young male respiratory doctor came in around 6 p.m. and gave us an update. Mom's lung capacity was severely diminished, and it was unclear if it was due to her lung being collapsed or the advancement of her COPD. He spoke to us about a procedure to re-inflate her lung that might improve her lung capacity and her ability to breathe. He patiently explained the risky procedure to us and then asked my mom what she wanted to do. To my utter surprise, she kindly told the doctor that she didn't want the procedure. And then she asked me what I thought. I agreed with her. She had been ill for a long time and fiercely fought for her life, and I supported whatever decision she made. "Whatever you want, Mom, I'll support you." I said.

* * *

"I won't wake her up."

I heard John's emphatic voice.

It took me a moment to wake up and come back to the room.

"I'm not going to wake her up."

I heard it again. This time, I jumped out of bed.

"Is Mom okay?" I said.

"She's okay, Babe, but there's big drama at the hospital. Supposedly Isabella thinks that you convinced your mom to not have some medical procedure last night, and she's all upset about it and how you want your mom to die and has been demanding to speak to you."

John covered the receiver of his phone. I heard my sister screaming on the other end.

I extended my hand.

"All I did was support Mom's decision," I said.

Isabella was furious. I got all kinds of grief for not consulting her. She was sure that Mom hadn't understood that she might die without the procedure.

Thankfully, in Isabella's mind the doctor had come back to make sure that Mom didn't want the treatment. I kept trying to explain that it was Mom's decision, and eventually I was yelling, too. I hung up and burst into tears.

I fell into John's arms. "Here we go again," I said.

This had happened with my dad, too. My family wanted to try every medical option and all it did was extend his suffering, and every night for a whole month I was the one with him, holding him as he screamed in pain – and none of the others were there with me to help.

"I can't go through that again, John, not with Mom. I just can't," I said and the tears rolling down my face.

John comforted me as I cried. "So what's happening now?" he asked.

"They're moving forward with the procedure in about an hour," I said. "Isabella wants me to come back to the hospital. There is a chance that Mom won't make it, but I'm not going. I'm wiped out. I've said my goodbyes to Mom and we're in a good place, and I just can't be there right now. I don't know what I'll do if she actually dies from this. I'm going back to sleep."

I climbed back into bed.

"Are you sure, Diana? I can drive you back and stay with you for as long as it takes," John said.

"I'm sure," I said. "If this is how they want Mom to die, then they can all deal with it. I'm out."

But the tears rolled down my face. I covered myself with the blankets and little Sophia jumped up on the bed and snuggled her furry face next to me. I heard John back on the phone again as he explained that I wasn't returning to the hospital. I struggled to go back to sleep.

* * *

A few hours later, I awoke to an exhausted John. Various family members had been calling and demanding that he take me to the hospital, that my mom was asking for me and that I wasn't being rational, etc., etc.

"Easy for them to say that when they don't stay with her through the night and see her suffering up close and personal for hours on end," I said. "Thanks for supporting me, Babe. I guess if she's asked for me, I better go to see her."

I took a quick shower and got dressed.

At the hospital, Mom was sleeping and Isabella was in her room.

"How did it go?" I asked.

"It didn't work, but she's okay," Isabella said. "Turns out her lung wasn't collapsed, it's the diminished capacity. But we had to try."

Isabella stood directly in front of me with her hands on her hips. "I can't believe you wouldn't come. She could have died and you would have never seen her again."

"And I can't believe you put her through this and it might have killed her."

Clearly this wasn't a shining moment for either of us, but I tried to remind myself that we were both dealing with what we both knew: Mom was dying.

Hospital stay — fourth night

"He made me come back because you were here," Mom said.

The sternness in her weak voice startled me.

"What are you talking about, Mom?" I said. "Who made you come back? Where were you?"

I wasn't sure she was fully awake.

"I was in the tunnel, Diana," Mom said. "I heard the most beautiful music I'd ever heard and I felt so good and I was so happy, and then he told me that I had to go back, and here you are even when I told you to go home."

Mom was shaking her head from side to side.

"Sorry, Mom, but I don't think I was the reason you were sent back. Who do you think sent you back?" I said.

"I think it was Jesus," Mom said. "I was so peaceful and so happy. And I could have gone home tonight if you hadn't been here."

"Was it opera, chant, symphony music?" I said.

"I had never heard music like it, and I have no way of describing what it sounded like, but it was the most beautiful thing I'd ever heard."

"Did you see the light? The bright one that

everyone always talks about?" I said.

"No, I don't remember super bright light. I was in a tunnel of some sort and it was so peaceful and the music, the music was so amazing." She was smiling. "Do you believe me?"

"Yes I do, Mom. I know that we go home and I think it is so awesome that you were fortunate to have a glimpse of it. But clearly, you still need to be here or he wouldn't have sent you back, and I'm not owning that I caused your return."

I smiled warmly as I held her hand. "Can you imagine how wealthy we'd be if I really could stop death, Mom? I could go from room to room and offer my services for a huge fee to keep patients alive."

"Ay, Diana, you would never charge anyone, you are so kind-hearted."

"You're probably right, Mom."

In the morning, they told us Mom would need to enter hospice. "For palliative care," the nurse said as she spoke to Isabella and me. "There's nothing more we can do."

"How long?" I asked.

"Three days."

Chapter Two

The Will of Love

A medical or grief expert gives you a time frame of how long your loved one has left, and sadly the death-watch begins.

It's hard for you to accept that you have only precious days left to spend with your loved one, and it's even harder to think about anything else.

You soon realize that death has its own schedule, and truly no one knows for sure when it will arrive.

There's never been a better time to accept this final journey and cherish these last days.

Day 1, Tuesday, Dec. 14, 2010

The hospice coordinator was waiting for me when I arrived at Mom's house to prepare for her last days. The nurse greeted me with a hug, and even though she was a complete stranger, it was comforting. I cried briefly as we stood in Mom's driveway, and it was a relief to talk about how hard all this was. I couldn't believe that our lives had taken such a rapid turn down the halls of my greatest fear, and it was my job, right now all alone, to get the house ready for Mom to die at home. For the past 24 hours, I'd focused on consoling my sons and my extended family, so much so that I hadn't stopped to acknowledge the grief I felt in every cell of my body.

The nurse explained that hospice would help us make Mom's final few days comfortable. This translated to new medication to help her breathe easier, manage her pain, anxiety, and on and on. Mom would also need to wear her Darth Vader mask to help manage her blood's carbon dioxide levels. The nurse handed me brochures on grief to distribute to our entire family, including my sons. I noticed one on the final stages of death, and tears filled my eyes again even though I heard the voice in my head saying, "Be strong, you knew this day would come." I did know, but it felt way worse than I'd feared.

Last, she gave me a list with phone numbers for the in-home equipment Mom would need. I sat in Mom's living room on her recliner and placed my first call to order the hospital bed and tray. I looked into her bedroom as I spoke on the phone and realized that she would never again be able to sleep in her comfy bed with her beloved yorkies, Gigi and Lulu. About 45 minutes later, a nice young man delivered the hospital equipment to our door, before I'd even finished with all the other phone calls. He set up her bed and walked me through the various settings. I was in a daze and completely overwhelmed. Thankfully I'd been a project manager in the early years of my career and those skills took over — lists, calls, tasks with deadlines — and I powered through everything. By mid-afternoon, Mom's house was ready.

Back at the hospital, I returned to spend the night with Mom, only to find my cousin Maria seated outside in the hallway. "You need to tell them to leave," she said, referring to about 20 family members, including nieces, nephews and cousins. "They've been here for hours and your mom needs to rest. And they haven't seen her for so long, and they don't deserve to see her now, like this. Go in, tell them to leave."

"Maria, I know that Mom wants to say goodbye to everyone," I said.

"They're just here to get gossip," she groused.

Maria was Mom's niece and her best friend. They'd been fiercely close since their days in the tuberculosis sanitarium – more than 60 years. They knew each other's biggest secrets and spoke to each other daily.

"I'll go check, but I think everyone is entitled to say their farewells, Maria," I said. "It's Mom, that's the way I know she wants it. She doesn't hold grudges."

I hugged Maria when I saw her tears.

Stepping inside, I entered a room full of family and friends that far exceeded visitor hospital policies.

"Isabella," I whispered, "should we make them take turns?"

But my sister explained none of the hospital staff would say anything, given that Mom had less than 72 hours to live.

For Mom, it had been years since she'd seen some of her family, but there was no guilt or shame about the missed birthdays or holidays: Mom was happy and I could see it. I returned to the hallway and told Maria, "Mom is happy, and that's all that matters right now."

Back at Mom's side, I listened as she told her visitors about her near-death experience and her upcoming journey home. She couldn't wait to see her mother, sisters, brothers and our father. Her coughing spells and labored breathing frightened some of the children, but she just powered through. My heart was breaking while I witnessed my dearest mama meet death with grace and gratitude. She was dying just as she'd lived.

Privately, relatives had asked me how long Rose had. They had been surprised to hear that it was just a few days. It was hard to process when you looked at her. Mom was alert and had no memory retrieval issues, only these horrible coughing spells.

After the room cleared out, I welcomed our last hospital night together. As I massaged her legs and arms, I fought back tears. I'd spent so many nights with her in Marian hospital and always in a place of "she'll be better soon." This was a new reality to understand. There were no more questions about her getting better. We had now officially entered into what had loomed over us, the death-watch phase.

The next morning, I triumphed in the battle with the hospital about how we would get Mom home. The doctors had recommended that we take her home, but with Mom's need for oxygen, inability to walk and continual coughing spells, it was going to be impossible to get her into a car and into the house. I pleaded with the hospital staff and finally had to threaten a lawsuit if anything happened to her while we tried to get her home. I didn't want us to take her home and have her break her hip, or something worse, because we dropped her.

An ambulance picked her up about 11 a.m. The paramedics were gentle, kind and respectful as they moved her onto the stretcher. Mom was delighted to be going home.

I checked the closet one last time and the hospital bed to ensure that we had everything: Mom's glasses, hearing aids, and flowers. It was a surreal experience to know that I would never again be staying with her in the "Marian Resort," as I jokingly had called it for so many years.

The paramedics arrived at Mom's small, comfortable home and transported her to the hospital bed. "I love this, Mia," she said as she tenderly looked up at me.

"I thought you'd like being in the living room, close to the sliding glass door so you could look out the window and watch the birds," I gently replied.

"I do, I love watching the birds," she said with a gentle smile and a little twinkle in her eyes.

It was also going to be easier for Mom's guests to visit her in the living room.

"What's going on with your job, Mia?" Mom asked me as soon as the paramedics left.

"It's all good, Mom. I was supposed to be on vacation in a few days anyway, and this is our slow time of the year. I've spoken to my boss a few times and it's fine, Mama. Please don't worry about my job right now."

"And what about the boys' school?" she went on.

"It's the end of the year, Mom. School is out now for the Christmas holiday, so they are fine for now, too."

Then, trying to change the subject, I said cheerfully, "Mom, it's almost Christmas. Do you want me to make you some pozole?"

"Oh, Mia, I'd love that." A slight smile brightened her face.

"Wonderful, I'll make it tomorrow. We can invite the family over too, because you know that your recipe makes pozole for about 50," I said.

"That will be so nice," she said, and squeezed my hand.

I finally summoned the courage to ask the question I'd been dreading all day. "Mom, do you want me to help you plan your funeral?"

"Yes. I have savings to cover everything," she said. "There are at least two mortuaries you should check out and I want lots of beautiful music at my mass." She spoke to me in her master chef voice as if she were instructing me on how to perfect one of her most complicated recipes, and I knew that this is how she was coping with this dreaded task.

"Okay, Isabella will be here tomorrow morning to take care of you, so I will get an early start and go to the mortuaries and shop for our pozole." My voice sounded fine, but I knew I spoke with a heavy heart. I knew that I'd be going to the mortuaries alone; no use in asking anyone to join me. This was a duty reserved for the oldest daughter, and they'd make excuses about it being too hard for them to deal with.

Gabriel and Jessie were staying at Isabella's house and came by for a little while to visit their grandmother before we went to bed for the night. It was so good to see them. I felt their stress and fear as they shyly spoke to their grandmother.

When we had told them Rose had only a few days left, they vehemently argued that she always got better. This was different, though. They were seeing her at home, in a hospital bed and not able to walk.

They knew she was in hospice. All this made it harder for them to deny it.

Before she went home for the evening, Isabella taught me how to wire the oxygen tubing into Mom's Darth Vader mask and breathing machine. But to say that I was completely a nervous wreck about the whole thing was such an understatement. If I wired the tubes incorrectly it could cause her carbon dioxide levels to get too high, causing her to fall into a coma, or even worse die. Oh, I wished I understood medical procedures and palliative care a little better!

It had been a big day, and Mom was tired. I started getting her ready for bed. I gave her a sponge bath, emptied her catheter, applied lotion to her body and helped her brush her teeth. She took her pain meds and a sleeping pill with some yogurt. I started adjusting her army of pillows into the perfect spots to help her get comfortable. Some of them went under her legs, feet, shoulders, etc. It was a puzzle to get it just right.

I had saved the hard part for the end. There was nothing left to do but deal with the terrifying Darth Vader mask and all the tubing. The last step required me to remove the oxygen from her nasal cannula and rewire it so she was completely without any oxygen for a few minutes. I was shaking and oh, so nervous.

"It will be okay, Mia, I can be without my oxygen for a few minutes," she gently said as I removed her oxygen nasal cannula. I wired it all exactly how Isabella had explained and double-checked my notes on my phone. I placed the mask on her face and ensured that it covered her nose and mouth and the straps were secured around the top of her head. I turned it on and it seemed to be working. Mom signaled it was okay.

"You promise, you'll call me if you need anything," I said as I tucked in her blankets. "I can sleep on the sofa."

"I will call you, and you need to sleep in the bed, Mia." She struggled to speak from behind her mask.

"Okay, but I'm going to stay here until you're asleep and then I'll go to bed," I said. "*Que duermas con los angelitos (sleep with the angels)." I looked into her eyes and blessed her forehead with the sign of the cross. This was a blessing that my mother had given me countless times, and now it was my turn to give it to her.

I had a restless night. I kept waking up to check on Mom. I was so concerned that I'd wired her oxygen tubing incorrectly. About 4 a.m. I got up to check on her again. Her air compressor hummed loudly, her mask still securely on her face. She looked so uncomfortable with the giant white machine over her face, her body rigid and unable to lie on her side and only stay on her back. There wasn't anything peaceful about this image of my sweet mama.

Day 2, Wednesday, Dec. 15, 2010

About 7 a.m., I heard her start moving around.

"Good morning, beautiful Mama," I said as I gently stroked her forehead.

Her eyes blinked slowly, and she pointed at the mask. I walked around the bed to the side with the control box and gently started removing it. When I removed the mask, Mom's face was constrained. Red lines marked where the edges of the mask had compressed against her cheeks and nose.

"Okay, just need to get your oxygen back into your nose, and you're all good," I said as I placed the oxygen nasal cannula in her nostrils.

"Thank you, Diana. I know you didn't sleep," she said all too knowingly as she looked up at me.

"I was worried that I wouldn't hear you if you needed something. But I have a plan. I'm going to get you a bell today, so you can ring if you need anything. Just like a very important person at a fancy hotel."

Mom smiled. "Okay, let's give it a try".

Mom was still able to sort out all her medications. I gave her the box with all the bottles. Even though she was in hospice, she was still taking her meds for high blood pressure, diabetes, etc., all to keep her comfortable. There were more than 20 pills taken at different times throughout the day, some with food and some without. There were breathing treatments, inhalers and pain meds, but she had it all memorized.

"I'd never be able to keep all those pills straight, Mama. I need a phone app," I said as I gave her some decaf coffee and she had a banana.

"Ay, Mia, you and your phone, it's not hard to remember. I've been doing it for years. You'd remember if you had, too," she said as she looked up at me.

Isabella arrived around 10 a.m. I was showered and ready to start my big morning of errands. My first stop was St. Louis de Montfort Catholic Church. The morning masses were over, and I quietly snuck in through one of the side doors. I knelt down in the pew, made sure no one was watching and slipped a music missalette into my large purse. I needed it to help Mom pick the music for her funeral, and hopefully I'd be forgiven for this misdemeanor.

Next stop, Dudley-Hoffman Mortuary. They had handled my father's services in 1994. It was the largest mortuary in town and was nicely decorated with soothing funeral music playing as entered the front door.

A funeral director greeted me politely at the reception desk and led me into his office. He handed me a large green folder and began to slowly explain all its contents including the various fees, picking up her remains, preparing them for viewing, embalming, and re-opening my parents' plot. It was surreal to have this conversation about my beautiful mama, and I struggled to hold back tears and pay attention. I thought of all the other people who had sat in this chair answering these questions, and their heartache as they tried to plan their loved one's burial.

After I'd reviewed all the paperwork I asked to see the coffins. He took me into a large room with about 10 rows of elegantly displayed open caskets. He explained that there were dresses and gowns on a rack if we were interested in clothing too. He also showed me custom pillows, inserts, etc. "I'll leave you alone for you to explore," he said as he headed toward the door.

"One last question," I said. "Can I take pictures of the coffins so I can show my mom?"

"Of course, take as many as need and stay as long as you like," he replied as he left the room and closed the door.

Alone in the room with funeral music playing in the background, I felt my heart pounding and tears began to stream down my face immediately. My thoughts went back to those other families that had come to this room before me and those who were to come. I was aware of the sadness and raw grief that had passed through here, and today was my turn.

I walked around and took photos of the various caskets. I noticed a beautiful rose-colored casket with an image of the Virgen de Guadalupe embroidered on the top inside lid. Mom had a soft spot for the Virgen and this color, so I thought this might be the one.

When I returned home, Mom slept wearing her mask. Isabella went home, and I started cooking the pozole. Mom and I had been making this traditional Mexican soup with pork and hominy together since I was a child. It was usually the main entree for our large New Year's Eve celebrations and one of my mother's most complex recipes with a total prep and cooking time of about seven hours. Even though I'd made it by myself a few times before, this time it had to be the very best as it would most likely be the last time my sweet mama would enjoy one of her favorites.

As I looked at her small, highly functional kitchen I thought about all the times we'd cooked here together, side by side. I knew where everything was, her knives, cutting boards, pots and her molcajete. I briefly wished I had my Grandma Magdalena's magical molcajete, but it was in my kitchen, sitting on the counter by my stove where'd it been for the last 15 years. I used it all the time to crush garlic and spices, and I was convinced that it made my recipes taste amazing!

As I rinsed Mom's molcajete, I knew that this one had some magic, too. Mom had been using it for over a decade, and it was filled with all the love she put into her recipes.

I put on her 49er apron and cut up the large 12-pound pork shoulder into three-inch cubes. Then I peeled three heads of garlic, placed them in mom's molcajete added a little sea salt, and picked up the tejolote with my right hand and began to pound the garlic. As I ground the tejolote against the basalt rock of molcajete, my ears welcomed the familiar sound, a drumbeat that was almost like a heartbeat, and I had the garlic crushed in a few minutes. I chopped two large onions. In one pan, I started boiling the pork shoulder, and in another, I cooked the pork feet. They both needed to boil for at least three hours. In a third pot, I began the process of rehydrating the dried Pasilla, California, Guajillo and New Mexico chiles that would give the pozole its deep red color and make it spicy.

Looking at Mom's brown gas stove, I was delighted that it was once again busy creating the magic that we had experienced so many times together.

From the living room, I heard Mom waking up, and I rushed to her hospital bed. "Are you ready for me to remove your mask?" I asked as I gently held her hand.

She nodded quickly, yes. "Oh, Mia, it smells so good. It woke me up. You've started cooking the pozole."

"It should be ready around 7:30 p.m. Do you want me to invite everyone to come over?" I raised up her bed and started adjusting her pillows.

"Yes, I'd love that, Mia," she said.

I managed to get her to eat a little lunch. As we talked, the house continued to fill with the aromas of the pozole. It was heavenly, comforting and so very familiar.

"Mom, I went to Dudley's and Moreno mortuaries today," I said "They gave me details about their services and I took photos of the caskets at Dudley's. Do you want to take a look at everything?"

To my surprise, Mom said in her weak voice, "Yes, Mia, let's look at it. I don't think Moreno's has a room big enough for my rosary, what do you think?"

I handed her two folders. "It's pretty small, and they have just one viewing room. They also don't keep any caskets in stock. We'd need to order a casket from a catalog without seeing it. But they're much cheaper than Dudley's."

Mom carefully reviewed both estimates. "There's a charge to reopen our plot? And a cement liner, what's that?" She looked up from the Dudley estimate.

"You'll be buried on top of daddy separated by about three feet of dirt. And your casket will be placed into the cement liner to keep the ground from sinking as the coffin decomposes," I calmly explained.

"I've been saving for this, Mia, and I have enough money to cover all the costs. I wanted to compare and understand the differences. I've been to a couple of rosaries at Moreno's, and it's small with no parking." She looked up again.

"We have to give hospice the name of your preferred mortuary by tomorrow," I reminded her.

"Do either of them need any money up front?" she asked as she carefully handed me the folders.

"No. The full payment is required following all the services." So far, so good, but it was a challenge to remain calm and helpful.

"May I see the pictures of the caskets?" she said.

I leaned down to show her the casket photos on my phone. Her strength and focus astounded me. There was no sadness, no anger, just purpose.

"Oh, Mia, I like this pretty rose one," she said. "What do you think?"

"That's my favorite, Mom," I said. "I thought you might like that one, too."

"Is it expensive?" She was spreading her thumb and forefinger out, trying to enlarge the picture and get a closer look.

"It's one of the cheaper ones," I said.

"That's the one, Mia, the pretty rose one," she said, like it was the final big choice of her lifetime. She looked away for a moment, and I went to check on my boiling pozole pots. I knew that she'd seen many caskets in her lifetime with her loved ones laid out: her parents, all her sisters, her brothers, her best friends, my father.

A few minutes later when I returned to the living room, she was looking out the window.

"Are you okay?" I gently asked.

"Yes, Mia," she said. "Thank you for going to the mortuaries. I know that no one else could have done this alone, and I appreciate you doing this for me."

"Of course, Mom." That was all I could get out. I was unable to say anything else. My heart ached for what was coming. The end of this closeness, this connection we had, and the only way I could hold back the tears was to say almost nothing.

I escaped to the kitchen again to regroup, check on the pozole, while Mom watched TV.

About 30 minutes later, I returned to her side with the church hymnbook.

"Mom, look what I have," I said mischievously as I held it up.

"Ay, Diana, what did you do? Did you steal that from St. Louis De Montfort?" Mom said a little disapprovingly.

"Nope. I borrowed it for the next 24 hours, so we can select your music for the mass," I said as I handed it to her.

She formed a little grin as she took it from me. She flipped through it and handed it back to me. "Will you help me?"

I sat down next to her and suggested a few hymn names, but they weren't resonating with her. Next I read a few lines of the lyrics, and that didn't do it for her, either. So I started singing.

"And I will raise him on eagles' wings ..."

"Ay, Mia, I didn't know you couldn't sing," she said, laughing at my poor attempt.

"Really Mom, here I am trying to help you and you're going to make fun of me," I said. "I think that might be a sin."

We giggled like schoolgirls. We struggled through my singing and managed to select five beautiful songs, including "Ave Maria." I promised to return the missalette the following day. It felt good to have this task completed. I entered the song titles into my phone so I wouldn't misplace them.

"It's going to be beautiful. I love music," she said with a sense of accomplishment.

"Yes, it is, Mom," I replied. "Just gorgeous."

"I'm glad we're getting everything ready, Mia, but I plan to stay alive until Renee's baby is born," she said with great conviction. Mom had tremendous faith and prayed the rosary every day, and usually included intentions and prayers for our large extended family. This was one of the first times I heard her reference praying for something she wanted. "I have to meet my first great-granddaughter, and I'm praying that God will grant me this last wish."

"I'll pray for that too, Mama." Tears welled up in my eyes.

She was tired, and I put the mask back on her and she quickly went to sleep. I returned to our pozole. I removed the pork shoulder and the pork feet from both pots and combined the stocks into one extra large stockpot. After washing the canned hominy, I added it to the stockpot to simmer for about 90 minutes.

For most of my life, using canned hominy wasn't an option because Mom was convinced that it would degrade the flavor of her pozole. She was a complete snob about her superior, "all-from-scratch" pozole compared to other relatives who used canned hominy.

Preparing homemade hominy from dried corn kernels was a tedious, backbreaking event. The cooking process of soaking, boiling the corn with CAL (pickling lime), washing and simmering it took hours. The CAL helped loosen the corn kernels hulls (outer layer) and it could only be completely removed by repeated hand washing and kneading of the corn. Once clean and hull free the corn was simmered for hours again so that it could fully open up and doubled in size.

My repeated attempts to persuade her to use canned hominy and simplify her recipe failed for years. But as her health declined she had loosened her standards and she said it was okay to use canned hominy because they'd really improved the quality and it was finally as good as hers.

While the hominy simmered and the kitchen aromas comforted me I began to work on the chiles. They had cooled and were soft. I placed them in the blender with onions and garlic and strained them to remove the seeds. The bright, brick-red chile paste that remained after blending and straining looked just like Mom's. I added about half of it into the hominy pot, mixed together and let the flavors magically combine.

With the challenging steps behind me, I quickened my pace and made salsa, guacamole, and chocolate cupcakes filled with cream cheese.

Mom woke up about an hour before everyone was scheduled to arrive for dinner. I removed her mask, brushed her hair and tidied her up for her guests.

"Did you make cupcakes, Mia? I smell them," Mom asked with a little twinkle in her eye.

"And no, you can't have one before dinner," I said as I helped get her into a nice clean nightgown.

"I'll still eat dinner," Mom pleaded like a 4-year-old.

"If you eat a little pozole, I'll give you a cupcake," I said as I caved.

I returned to the kitchen to chop all the condiments for the pozole: fresh onion, radishes, cilantro, cabbage and limes. "Mom, can you taste this for me?" I said as I held a spoonful of cooled pozole broth by her bed.

Her eyes got big as she looked at the spoon, "Oh, yes, Mia, it smells so good." She opened her mouth and I fed her the pozole. "It's so good, Mia. But it needs salt, a little oregano and maybe some more pepper."

Back to the kitchen, I added the ingredients. Then it was back to Mom for another taste test. This back-and-forth continued for another three times, until Mom said it was perfect.

I gave her a small bowl of pozole, and she was able to feed herself.

"Oh, Mia, this is the best pozole I've ever eaten," she said. "It's even better than mine."

"Thank you." For a moment I considered reminding her that I used canned hominy, but instead I let the words linger there. I knew I would forever cherish this memory of our last pozole.

At last, I said, "Are you ready for your cupcake?"

I removed her bowl from the table, though I knew her answer before she spoke.

Mom ate her cupcake slowly. She gently removed the wrapper. She took small bites and savored every morsel.

"We've been making these for a long time, Mom. Do you remember when I taught you how to make them? I think I was 13 when Olivia Warner taught me the recipe and then I taught you."

She took a break from her cupcake. "Yes, but then I changed the recipe to use a box cake mix instead of the one from scratch, and then it became my recipe." She had set the record straight.

I smiled. "Oh, Mom, that doesn't make it your recipe. It's a new version, but not a whole new recipe."

"Nope, not the way I see it."

Back in the kitchen, knowing people would arrive soon, I put the finishing touches on our feast. Mom was the most loving, forgiving woman I'd ever known, but her recipes brought out a whole other persona. She should have been a chef, and I'm sure she would have been wildly successful.

Sol and Emelio Gomez and their children, our dearest friends, were first to arrive. My parents had helped them become U.S. citizens some 40 years ago when they first emigrated from Mexico, and they had become part of our family. They were living in Mexico again, but we stayed close and their family had claimed my mother, too. This was Mom's way — Mama to so many. Mom's eyes lit up when they came into the living room to greet her with their warm smiles, hugs and sweet kisses on the cheek.

Peter and his family arrived next. By official bloodlines he was my nephew, but he was officially a wonderful brother. He and his younger sister had come to live with us when he was only 4 years old and Mom had raised them both.

He ushered me to the garage and shyly offered to help us financially with anything Mom needed. He'd done very well for himself and had a successful business. "I'm really busy and I will come to visit as often as I can, but I won't be able to take care of her," he continued.

I knew him well and understood that he couldn't watch her die. He loved her so much and it was too much for him. Peter's mother had abandoned him, and Mom was his rock. He had been so good to Mom his whole life and I appreciated his love and honesty. I hugged him and we returned to the kitchen.

My sons, sisters and oldest brother arrived a little later. Mom's little house was filled with more than 30 friends and relatives. Everyone loved the pozole, salsa, guacamole and cupcakes. The Gomez family commented about how much they loved my mother's cupcake recipe, and I just let it go. Oh, that mother of mine.

"Your pozole is the best we've ever had," the Gomezes said. "Quite an accomplishment for someone not born in Mexico!"

"The master chef taught me," I said. "She completed the final taste testing and recipe adjustments to get it to this level of perfection."

Later, the house filled with love and food and family, I huddled with Isabella and asked: "Do you think she really only has one day left?"

I hadn't noticed another big decline. She coughed all the time and was very tired, but it was hard for me to believe that death was so near.

"It's just an estimate, Diana," Isabella said.

My sister went on to explain the medical view, but I was barely listening: Doctors don't really know. Everyone is different. Some patients can be released from hospice a few weeks after they were given a few days to live. Some improve. She continued on, but it was clear that she didn't want to discuss this any further, and I was not sure I wanted to hear more.

Late in the evening, I walked my sons out to say good night. When I came into the living room, I overheard Mom asking Sol Gomez to pray for her. "I know my time is close, but I really want to be here to meet my very first great-granddaughter."

Sol promised to pray for her, just as I had. Mom would need to live for another four months to meet her first great-granddaughter, who was due in spring. Right then, standing on the porch, I prayed for a miracle.

Day 3, Thursday, Dec. 16, 2010

I woke up to an insistent, ringing bell. Instantly, I ran to her hospital bed. Mom was tugging at her mask and noticeably panicking. I quickly removed it, and she was coughing uncontrollably. I raised up her bed to see if that would help with the coughing, but it didn't. She put down her tissue and grabbed another one. It was full of blood.

Grabbing the phone, I called Isabella. "Stay calm," she said. "It's probably because of all the coughing."

After a long five minutes, Mom's coughing spell subsided and she spoke, feebly. "I couldn't breathe,

Mia. It was so scary. I just couldn't catch my breath, and I held it for as long as I could. But I couldn't cough in the mask. I'm so sorry I woke you up so early. You look so tired."

"You aren't bothering me, Mom," I said. "I felt so helpless. I couldn't help you." Tears welled in my eyes as I held her hand.

"Bring me some water, Mia," Mom said with slow, labored breaths.

The hospice nurse arrived about an hour later and took Mom's vitals. Mom told her about her terrifying coughing spell, and the nurse suggested she sleep with her back a little higher. The Darth Vader mask helped her carbon dioxide levels but didn't help with Mom's excessive phlegm production. She was going to get Mom another breathing treatment to help keep the phlegm loose and easy for Mom to expel.

After the medical evaluation, the nurse sat on the sofa and explained that she'd be one of her nurses. "I'll come to visit you every other day," she said. "You can ask me anything."

She stood to hug Mom. Noticing all the saints by Mom's bed, she said she would be praying for her.

Before she left, the hospice nurse handed me a magnet for Mom's refrigerator with the hospice phone number and instructed me to call anytime with any concerns. She hugged me and quietly left. I was in awe of this angelic caregiver's patience, energy and presence.

I settled into my routine for the day, starting my work in the kitchen.

"What are you doing, Diana? It's only 10 o'clock in the morning," Isabella said as she came into the kitchen.

"Today, I will make Mom's Sonora enchiladas," I said, and it came out brittle. I hadn't meant to sound like that. "Bad morning" was all I could say.

We still had all the pozole.

"Oh, how you love to work," Isabella said.

"I can't help Mom right now, I can't make her better, all I can do is make the food she loves."

Then I choked up.

Chapter Three

The Nurse and the Home Chef

My heart goes out to you.

Your emotions will race up and down

as you try to care for your loved one.

Nothing prepares you for the pain you will

witness and endure.

In time, you'll fall into a routine

and it will become more manageable.

Be patient with your life right now,

and with yourself.

Day 5, Saturday, Dec. 18, 2010

"Honey, wake up!" John gently stroked my left shoulder. "Your mom is ringing her bell."

I jumped out of bed. From her hospital bed in the living room, Mom waved her hands, signaling for me to take off her mask. Her eyes were enormous with fear as she tried to catch a breath.

"I'm going as fast as I can, Mom," I said as I removed the mask and got her nasal cannula. I raised the bed and rubbed her back as she hacked away. As much as I tried, I couldn't stop my tears. It broke my heart to see her struggle to breathe.

After about five minutes, she stopped coughing. She looked up at me with her large frightened eyes filled with tears and took my hand. "It's terrifying, Mia, not being able to breathe."

"I can't even imagine, Mom."

I wiped the tears from my cheeks quickly, but she'd seen them.

"I've had a good life, Mia," she continued. "Isabella and you are the best daughters and you are both so good to me. I've always had food to eat, a roof over my head, I'm so grateful, Mia."

"I know, Mom, that's what you always say, be grateful, there are people without food, that don't have a place to live, no family, etc. But I just don't want you to suffer and be in pain."

I tried to stop crying, but the tears seemed to be coming directly from deep down in my heart and they continued to roll down my face.

"It's not up to us. He'll take me when I'm supposed to go. I just want a few more months so I can meet Renee's baby. This is what happens, you know this, Mia, we all have to leave and we don't get to choose how or when."

"But I think you've suffered more than your share, Mom," I said. "Tuberculosis, cancer, a heart attack and now COPD. It's way too much for you."

I knew that I sounded like a stubborn, self-righteous child.

"You can't think like that, Mia. We don't get to make those choices. I've survived all those illnesses and I'm 83 years old. I'd never dreamed that I'd live to be this old."

"I love you so much, Mom," I said, and though I felt helpless, I asked, "Is there anything I can do for you?"

"Cherish your life, Mia. Don't live with any hate in your heart."

I knew she was talking about my feelings about my sons' father.

"I don't hate him, Mom," I said. "I'm just not very fond of how he has treated me. He's left it to me to provide all the financial support for our sons and it's hard and it's scary. He has so much more education than me. And…"

I was on my soapbox. I stopped myself.

Mom gently took my hand, looked at me wisely and said, "You have to forgive him, Mia. This isn't good for you or my grandsons to continue to feel like this."

For a moment, my thoughts worked through me as I wanted to justify my inability to forgive him. Mom forgave everything and everyone – it was her way.

"You don't understand, Mom," I said finally. "Daddy always worked, always provided for us. I know that we were poor, but he milked cows 16 hours a day for us."

She looked at me sternly. "Listen to your mother, Diana. You must forgive him. I'm not saying that you need to get back together with him, but forgive him."

Then I said what she wanted to hear. "I will try, Mom."

* * *

I had a big day of cooking ahead.

I stood in Mom's kitchen at 5:30 a.m. It was dark, cold and damp. I couldn't turn on the heat because it made it harder for Mom to breathe, so I put on a warm sweatshirt.

First on the list was Mom's favorite breakfast food, chorizo and papas. I crumbled the chorizo into a large skillet. As it sizzled in the pan, I peeled potatoes and diced them. I added garlic and onion powder, red California chile powder, salt and pepper, and a little water to the chorizo as it browned. A few minutes later I added the raw potatoes and let the magic happen.

Mom wouldn't be ready to eat breakfast for hours, but once cooked, chorizo and papas could sit for a long time and be fine. I made enough for Isabella's family and my sons, who were still staying at their favorite aunt's house. I would call them later and ask them to join their grandma for breakfast. Everyone loved chorizo and papas.

Next up, chicken enchiladas. I rinsed the chicken breasts, placed them in a large pan, added fresh crushed garlic from the molcajete and onions. While the chicken was boiling, I started a pot with fresh Peruvian beans. Mom's little stove was humming away. The dark brown four-burner gas counter-top stove and matching hood were once again making culinary magic.

"Ay, Mia, what are you making? I smell chorizo and papas, frijoles, garlic," Mom said joyfully from the other room.

"It's a surprise, and you're going to love it," I said with a big smile as I stepped out of the kitchen doorway into the hallway near the living room so she could see and hear me.

"Are you going to make me try and walk to the kitchen to see what you're cooking?" Mom said, smiling back and shaking her head disapprovingly.

"I'm making chicken enchiladas. I took your yummy recipe and combined it with Tia Juve's, and I'm pretty sure you're going to love them. I made chorizo and papas too. Are you ready for a little breakfast?"

"You're such a good cook, Mia," she said. "But you should have gone back to bed. You look so tired. Are you going to call Isabella and everyone to come and have breakfast too?"

"Of course, but it's too early right now. I'll wait another hour and call them," I said.

"I'll wait so I can eat with them. But can I have a little taste of the chorizo and papas in a little spoon, and I'll take my pills with a banana," she said.

I went to the kitchen and returned with her requested sampling.

"Oh, Mia, this chorizo reminds me of my mother's. It is so good," she said as she took her spoonful. "I think it still needs some salt."

So began our taste-test ritual until she gave the chorizo her stamp of approval.

"I remember you sending me with dozens of your papas and chorizo burritos to all our after school 4-H activities," I told Mom. "You'd make me offer everyone a burrito. They all loved them and I never had any leftovers. But do you remember what they used to call me because of your burritos?"

"It was something kid," she said, smiling.

"They called me the Burrito Kid. I despised it because I was so chubby. And it was your delicious burritos fault." I was teasing her, of course.

"Oh Mia, they didn't call you that for very long," she said, dismissing my childhood struggle.

"Do you know that I was at Mervyn's recently and a woman yelled from across the aisle, 'Aren't you the Burrito Kid?'" I said. "It's still my nickname, Mom."

Mom laughed hysterically.

* * *

Surrounded by family, Mom struggled to finish a small corn tortilla with only two large tablespoons of chorizo, a little salsa, some cheese. It was mid-morning, and we all ate with Mom. I remembered that when she was healthy, she would have easily eaten two flour tortillas with about four times the chorizo. She had lost 15 pounds since she went into the hospital. She was tall at 5-foot-7, and at 140 pounds and large bone structure, she looked very thin and frail. It was going to be tough to keep her from losing more weight, but I was going to keep trying.

Through the day, Mom slept with her mask on while I finished up the chicken enchiladas, Peruvian beans and Spanish rice (orange rice). John brought us peach pies and ice cream. We were all set for another yummy dinner.

When Mom woke up about 5 p.m. from her nap, she was eager to hear about my progress in the kitchen.

"Tell me about your enchilada ingredients, Mia," she said. "I'm not sure I approve of you altering my recipe."

She looked longingly into the kitchen from her bed.

"I fried the corn tortillas and dipped them into the enchilada sauce, which had *crema (Mexican sour cream)* mixed in," I said. "Then I stuffed the tortilla with chicken, cheese and Ortega chiles. Tia Juvi doesn't fry her tortillas and you don't use crema."

"Give me a little bite."

I went back to the kitchen and heated up a small piece for her in the microwave.

"They're very good, Mia," she said as she chewed her tiny bite. "But..."

I waited for her master chef adjustment to perfection.

"... they need a little more cheese. The tortilla won't be so mushy when you bake it in the oven."

"Will do, Mom!"

"John bought us a peach pie and ice cream for dessert. The pie won't be as good as the ones you used to make," I said.

"We must have canned thousand jars of peaches," Mom added, smiling.

"I'll never forget the day daddy's goats climbed into your peach trees," I said. "We returned from Sunday Mass, to see your orchard under full attack by the fully grown white goats. I was about 6 years old and you looked like a professional baseball player as you went from tree to tree swinging the broom and knocking goats out of the trees. There were flying goats everywhere." I couldn't help but giggle.

"I told your father not to get goats, they eat everything, but he didn't listen to me," Mom said, seemingly still upset about the big goat escapade.

"Whatever happened to the goats?" I asked.

"We ate them and we never had goats again," Mom said.

Day 8, Tuesday, Dec. 21, 2010

"Why are you crying?"

Mom sat down with me in the pew at the back of the church.

"You're dead," I said, shocked that she didn't grasp the severity of the situation.

"Look at me, I'm breathing on my own without any oxygen. I no longer need to take a bunch of pills, and later today I get to see my mama, who I haven't seen for more than 40 years," she said.

I have to admit she did look adorable in her little hat, traveling clothes and suitcase.

"Come, let's go look at my body in the coffin," she said.

She sounded like a schoolgirl about to open a Christmas present early. I stayed back.

"I can't see you like that, Mom," I said.

Mom walked to the front of the church to inspect her remains. I stayed glued to my seat. After a few minutes, she walked back down the aisle and slipped in to sit next to me in the pew.

"The casket is so beautiful, Mia, but they put too much makeup on me," she said.

"Mom, you say that at every funeral."

It was quiet between us.

"Mia, don't be sad, look at me. I feel so good today and I'm so excited to see my mom, your dad, my brother and sisters."

"But I can't call you anymore, Mom."

* * *

From my bed, I could hear the whoosh of Mom's mask, and I knew she was still sleeping. Lulu, Gigi, and Sophia were awake, though, and they descended on me for tummy rubs.

Every day past the three-days-to-live prognosis was a bonus day and I knew I might wake up with her gone. It was unnerving. I had been living like that for years, the phone next to my bed, terrified that she'd get sick, die in her sleep. I was familiar with this emotional territory, the fear of losing my mother and my best friend. But this was a new level. The doctor had said three days. We were in hospice. A pamphlet on the final stages of death rested on the nightstand in my mother's room, where I slept now for these last days as she slept in her hospice bed in the living room. I consulted the pamphlet every day to check for signs.

When the hospice nurse arrived at 9 a.m., we had just finished our Darth Vader mask routine. This morning, it was even harder to get Mom to eat. She was able to eat only the banana.

So I asked the nurse privately: "I'm concerned about her lack of appetite."

We were on day ten.

"I know," the nurse said. "But that is just an estimate. I hate time frames, myself."

She explained that the hospice agency wasn't allowed to provide its services until a patient had less than six months to live. "Every patient is different. I'm surprised she's tolerating the mask."

Most patients stop using the mask after a few days, she explained, causing their carbon dioxide levels to accelerate and for them to die within a week. Loss of appetite and weight loss are big problems for end-stage COPD patients, she added.

Now I knew how I could help. If Mom was determined to meet her first great-granddaughter in March, there was something I could do to help her. I could make sure she kept eating, didn't lose weight and kept using the mask.

Maybe I wasn't a nurse like Isabella — I'm so inadequate when it came to all the medical stuff — but I knew how to cook more than a hundred of Mom's recipes. I would keep the food coming.

* * *

Mom had been watching the Lakers game for about 30 minutes when Gabriel and Jessie joined her. It only took one question from Gabriel, and Mom was off, sounding like an ESPN sportscaster as she gave the game highlights, the score, big plays, who was having a good game, who wasn't, who to look out for. She was alert and thrilled to be watching her beloved Lakers with her grandsons.

"Grandma is much better today," Gabriel said as left his grandmother for a few minutes and came into the kitchen to chat with me. "I don't think the doctors know anything."

"Yes, Gabriel, she seems better to me, too," I said. "But her nurses have assured me that she is gravely ill. We just don't know how much longer she will be able to hold on."

"Whatever, Mom, they don't know my

grandma," he said. "She will be okay, and you just like to worry."

If Mom did live longer, I was going to need to balance my life, work, and family with her needs. It was only four days until Christmas, and the boys would need to be with their father that day. My vacation time was running out. It was time to talk about Mom's long-term in-home care plan.

I wandered into the garage, where Isabella was doing laundry. "I'm going to have to go home, Isabella," I said, and explained the pressures of Christmas, work and co-parenting. "Unfortunately, I have to go back to work. I can't afford to take a leave of absence to take care of her."

"I know, Sis," Isabella said. "I'm not working right now so I can take care of her."

"I can come on the weekends and cook for her and give you a little break on Saturday and Sundays," I said, but I felt guilty that I couldn't do more.

"I wish I could tell you how long she has," Isabella said. "She's very ill, but it's Mom, and she's so darn determined that she is going to meet her great-granddaughter — and that's more than three months away."

That was our plan, and it was time to tell Mom. When Isabella and I came back into the living room to share our plan, Mom was sleeping. I silently asked the Virgen de Guadalupe to help my mama survive another three months. But I wondered how much more Mom would endure to last that long. She was thin and frail, and her nose and face had oozing open sores from the mask. The basic comforts I took for granted every day were already out of reach for her, like taking a shower, going to the bathroom or simply walking — all gone. But as I watched my mother sleeping, I saw only her strength, her faith, and her gratitude. To me, she seemed like a giant.

After her nap, I sat down next to her hospital bed and told her my plans. I was going home tomorrow morning and returning the day after Christmas with Gabriel and Jessie. My sons would be starting school in early January and I was going back to work. Isabella and I had worked it all out and she would be staying with Mom during the week I'd be coming on the weekends to cook for her for the entire week. As I spoke, Mom's face filled with worry.

"Oh, this will be too much for you girls," she said.

"We will be fine, Mom." I squeezed her hand.

* * *

Back in Redwood City, the four of us – John, myself and my sons had a quiet Christmas Eve. We played our traditional all-night Monopoly game and had a wonderful time. It was nice to spend a couple days with my sons in our home. My mama's health had taken a toll on them, too, and they talked a lot about how they knew she'd be up and around, making us all flour tortillas soon. It was hard to see Gabriel and Jessie unable to accept her terminal diagnosis, but I decided to let them come to terms with it on their own. There was no point in having an argument about their grandmother's impending death.

The day after Christmas, we returned to Santa Maria to find Mom doing about the same. She was so happy to see us, and Christmas was on. I had almost completed my Christmas shopping when Mom got sick in early December, so there were gifts. Isabella had put up her small table-size Christmas tree on the coffee table, and it made the entire room feel festive. Mom sat in her chair and opened her presents, like she had so many times before, expressing the joy of a small child. See's candy — nut and chews were her favorite — some nice nightgowns (her new full-time uniform), soft sheets for her bed, comfy towels and a bottle of perfume. She collected perfume, and always loved the pretty bottles. It was a bit of a yearly tradition.

When she was done opening presents, she looked up and said, "Did you forget something?"

"I'm sorry, Mama. I didn't have time to make it yet. I promise to make it for you soon."

I felt embarrassed. I'd been making her personalized calendars with photos of my sons and the rest of the family for the past 16 years. The look on her face said it all: I'm still here, treat me the same way.

Time for dinner: tamales, with Krispy Kreme doughnuts for dessert. "We bought the tamales from the amazing tamale lady in San Jose, and they're delicious," I said.

"Folded or tied?" she asked.

"Folded, but they're scrumptious," I said. "John, Gabriel and Jessie already ate a half dozen on the way here. They're not as good as yours, but I thought it would be nice to have tamales at Christmas like we have so many times before."

"Okay, I'll try one," she said. "*Rajas con queso,* if you have it."

To her surprise, she liked it. We reminisced about our tamale-making escapades as we ate with her in the living room. We used to make hundreds of tamales at Christmas. Chicken, pork mole, *rajas con queso*, potatoes, and carrots. She made them old school, and there was none of this folded tamales nonsense. We had to tie both ends with string.

We'd been making tamales together every year for as long as I could remember. It was a family tradition, and Mom's children and friends gathered for this cherished event. Last year we'd made them in her garage. It was a multiple-day ordeal, and she sat at the end of the giant assembly line of tamale masa, corn leaves, moles, rajas, cheese, carrots, potatoes and at least ten pairs of hands with her oxygen nasal cannula on, and inspected every single one.

She returned about 10 percent of the tamales to be reassembled because they were too big, too small, mole was leaking, etc. She was one tough tamale inspector, but we loved it – and her tamales were the best.

Day 17, Thursday, Dec. 30, 2010

Five days flew by, and it was time to return home.

I was working to complete the morning's rewiring effort of the nasal cannula when I told Mom we were going home. "Do you want me to make you pancakes for breakfast?"

"No, thank you, Mia. You have a long day ahead of you. I really appreciate all the cooking you've done for me."

"I'll send John to get us some fresh Mexican bread," I said deviously.

"Does he know to get me the *Elotes*?" she said approvingly with wide eyes and a big smile.

"Of course, Mama, they're my favorite, too."

"Mia, this is going to be too much for you. Your job, taking care of your sons, coming back and forth," she said sadly.

"I'll manage, Mom. And I promise if it gets to be too much I will tell you and we'll figure something out.

I just wish I didn't have to go home." Tears filled my eyes.

Before we packed up to leave, I walked all the dogs to the nearby grammar school and let them run in the tall grass. They reminded me of the lions in the movie *Born Free* as they scrambled, their ears flopping. I was going to miss Lulu and Gigi, and I knew Sophia was going to as well.

Now the car was packed, but I sat with Mom and waited for Isabella. Being on time wasn't her strength, but I knew the next week was going to be tough for her, too.

"Just go, Mia," Mom said, holding my hand. "The traffic is going to be bad, and I'll be fine until she gets here."

When Isabella arrived, for the first time ever I decided to not make a big deal about her being 20 minutes late. It seemed trivial given Mom's situation. I was pleasant and showed her all of the food. I had stored some in the refrigerator and more in the freezer, and there was enough for her family, too.

Gabriel and Jessie lingered in the kitchen, and I realized they were looking for the lunch bags Grandma used to make for their trip home. I tried to signal them to come back to the living room while I sorted out what to say to them about this absent tradition, but it was too late — Mom instinctively knew what they were looking for.

"Mia, get me my purse," I heard my mother call from the living room.

I stood at Mom's bedside as her hands worked through her purse to find her wallet. She handed them cash.

"I'm sorry I can't make you lunches today," she said. "But take this and have your mom stop and buy you a hamburger."

Gabriel and Jessie solemnly took the dollar bills from their grandma and kissed her goodbye. They were ashamed that they had reminded their sweet grandma that she could no longer make them lunches with their beloved burritos. My heart was breaking. Back home, we settled into our routines of work and school. Every morning and every evening, I called Mom. Most of the time she could speak to me for only a few minutes through the coughing.

I continued to fill her in on my day-to-day work challenges and my sons' various activities, and she still managed to listen and ask probing questions. Her body was failing, but she was still my same wise mama, the world's best listener.

Day 24, Thursday, Jan. 6, 2011

When Friday finally came, John and I packed up the car with Sophia and all the food I planned to cook for Mom and headed out of the Bay Area. My sons stayed with their dad, who lived only about two miles from us. The traffic was terrible, and it took us about six hours to get to Santa Maria, 50% longer than normal. But when we came through her front door about 11 p.m., Mom was still awake.

"Oh, Mia, I was worried about you, driving in the dark in the rain after working all week," she said as she took my hand.

My heart raced with joy and gratitude as I kissed her forehead. "John did all the driving, Mom, and my car knows the way to see my mama," I said.

"I brought some movies for us, Mom," I said. "One that I think you will love. We also stopped to get you Krispy Kreme doughnuts."

Her eyes got big. "Any lemon-filled bars?"

"Of course, I know that is your favorite."

I flipped back the lid to show her.

"I haven't taken my last sleeping and pain pills, Mia," she said. "Can I have half a lemon doughnut with my pills?"

She asked like a schoolchild. Isabella looked on and shook her head disapprovingly.

"You girls spoil me," she said between bites. Isabella kissed her and blessed her and left for the night, saying, "I'll be back on Sunday, Mom. But Diana knows to call me anytime if you need anything."

I walked Isabella to the front door to catch up for a few minutes.

"The coughing is scaring her and making her nervous and anxious," Isabella said. "She's taking more anxiety pills when she goes to bed at night and anti-depression medication. She may need half of an anxiety pill tomorrow."

My sister was stressed. Even with hospice nurses coming every other day, caring for Mom all week was taking its toll.

"I'm going to call the church tomorrow and see if we can get someone to come and bring Mom communion," I said. "Maybe that will help calm her."

There, that took care of Mom. Now, Isabella. I was in full-solution mode.

"And it might be time to get you some help, Isabella," I added. "I think Mom qualifies for in-home care support. I can start making calls for that, too."

"I don't think I need any help yet," was all Isabella said as she hugged me and left.

* * *

So many times I wished for the magic wand. I wished I could lift the burden from my sister. I wished I could stop the coughing. I wished my mother could get a breath of air.

That morning, Mom had a serious coughing attack.

"Oh, Mia, this is so much scarier than when I had tuberculosis," she said. "I can't get air in."

She held my hand and touched a finger to her chest.

"I wish I could make you better."

And then, when I was least expecting it, she said, "Do you really think I went in the tunnel, Mia?"

I shifted in my chair.

"Or do you think I just dreamed the whole

thing?"

She had been thinking about her near-death experience a lot. I had been thinking about it, too. I took a deep breath. I said a quick a prayer and asked for help with this sensitive conversation.

"I've been reading about the final stages of COPD, and the carbon dioxide levels causing you to hallucinate, etc. Do you really think heaven exists?" Mom continued.

I considered all of this. "Yes, I do. I know it does. And I'm sure that you're getting one of those gigantic corner suites with a beautiful ocean view." I smiled gently at her.

"Are you scared to die?" she asked.

"No, Mom, I'm not," I said. "I know there's more, and that my body is just a host for my soul, and someday I will go home to heaven, too. I'm hoping that I can live long enough to see Gabriel and Jessie all grown up. I wouldn't want to leave them when they are so young."

"It doesn't get easier to leave them when they're older," she said. I knew she was right, but I couldn't respond. Be strong, said the voice in my head. She needs your strength right now, not your tears.

"Aren't you excited to see your mom, daddy, brothers and your sisters?" I said.

"Do you really think I'm going to see them?" she asked.

"Yes, I do. I think they are going to be so excited to see you! You'll be going to parties for months."

That morning, I managed to get her to eat a banana with her pills and nothing else. I couldn't even bribe her with a doughnut. She watched TV for a while, then asked that I put her mask back on, whereupon she fell asleep immediately. I sat and watched her for a few minutes. I'd hoped that her exit would be quick and pain-free. She'd been so ill all her life. I used to tease her that she was like a cat with nine lives and how she must be close to exceeding her ninth one. But now ... now that we were experiencing her ninth one, I didn't like it one bit. I cherished these few moments with her alone.

Even with her poor health she had managed to be Mom to so many that it had been tough to get her all to myself. My father was a widower with five children when he married Mom. She had helped him raise his children. Mom had me first, then my younger brother Matthew, then Isabella. My half siblings were much older, and many of their children were closer to my age than they were. Mom's heart was always open to caring for their children, and thus our house always had grandchildren staying with us for extended periods. As her oldest daughter, this meant that I helped her a lot with caring and feeding everyone, and sometimes I resented having to share her. But now that I was older, I understood that my beautiful mama only knew how to share herself with everyone she met. And literally give you everything she had.

I returned to the kitchen and started making *albondigas*, Mexican meatball soup. First, I made the meatballs – the *albondigas* – by mixing hamburger and ground chicken, a little white rice, finely chopped onions, garlic, tomato sauce, bread crumbs, eggs, finely chopped cilantro. I let the meat set for a few minutes and started the broth. Fried onions, tomato sauce, celery, garlic and red peppers went in to flavor the broth.

At the ringing of Mom's bell, I left the kitchen and raced to her bedside. I removed her mask, and before I even put on her glasses she grabbed my hand.

"Oh, Mia, are you making *albondigas*?" she said with a little smile.

"Yes, I am," I said. "I even put in some *chayotes* (squash) and altered your recipe a little. So you'll have to taste it and see what you think."

"I've been craving soup, Mia," she said. "Thank you."

For lunch, I prepared a small bowl for her with a small slice of buttered French bread.

"It's so good, Mia," I said. "I haven't had these in so long. And the *chayotes* remind me of when my mother would make them for us."

"What do think of my changes to your recipe?"

I waited patiently for my master chef's critique.

"I love cilantro, Mia," she said. "It tastes very different without *yerba buena* (mint). It's a good alternative, Mia."

That night we watched *Dreamer*, and John brought Mom rocky road ice cream. "Oh, Diana, I loved that movie," and when she said it, she sounded like herself again. I got her ready for bed, and the longest part of the entire process was getting all her pillows just right. Poor mama was clearly very uncomfortable in her tiny hospital bed, but didn't complain about it. I gave her half an anxiety pill with her sleeping pill and pain medication, and she had a good night.

I woke up early Sunday morning and finished off Mom's menu for the week ahead: homemade chicken soup, orange rice and black beans. Isabella came over about 2 p.m. to resume her duties, and it was time to say goodbye. This was the hardest part of my entire visit, leaving her.

The next three weeks went by quickly. Isabella stayed with her during the week, and I came and stayed with her on the weekends. Mom was about the same except for the terrible sores on her face from the mask. The plastic seal that went around her nose and mouth irritated her skin. Isabella and the hospice nurses tried all kinds of things to keep her skin from breaking down, including soft cloths, facial tissue, lamb's fur, etc., but nothing seemed to work and Mom's sores just got worse.

Day 46, Friday, Jan. 28, 2011

"Did you remember to get the garbanzo beans?"

I was changing Mom's nightgown before breakfast. She knew that this weekend I was going to make beef *machaca*, but I had never made it alone.

It was a really complicated recipe that took hours to make and resulted in shredded spicy beef with garbanzo beans, onions, peppers, cilantro, garlic and tomatoes.

"Yes, Mom, I did," I said. "I've never tried to make this recipe before alone. I sure hope it comes out okay."

I immediately regretted that I said alone. I wasn't cooking alone. We were cooking together.

"I know, Mia, I wish I could cook with you," she said.

"I'm sorry, Mom. I know you can't. I wasn't thinking. And you are cooking with me. You're going to have to walk me through it, and I will just be your hands."

"It's okay, Mia, I know what you meant. I miss cooking the most, Mia, even more than taking a real shower. What I wouldn't give to be able to stand next to you in the kitchen in front of my stove."

"And how I would love that too, Mom."

On this day, I made numerous trips between her kitchen and hospital bed for taste tests and recipe tweaks. It needed cloves, cumin, more salt, more garlic, more cilantro. But oh, the final flavor was amazing. Even from a hospital bed, my mom was the best chef I'd ever known.

We watched the movie *Secretariat* after dinner, and I made homemade popcorn. We had a pleasant evening. I had almost forgotten that she was still terminally ill that day, and it was a gift.

I made her some *calabacitas (Mexican squash)* on Sunday, fresh orange rice and pinto beans. My heart ached again knowing that I'd be leaving in a few hours to go home. And this time, we would change the schedule again.

I would have to start coming on Saturdays, rather than Fridays. The traffic was too heavy on Fridays.

"So I'll probably do some of your cooking at my house and some here so I can keep you stocked up for the week," I explained to Mom. "I spoke to Isabella and she's okay with it."

"Oh, Mia, that's okay," Mom said. "I've been so worried about you driving on Friday nights. Of course I'd love to see you more, but I understand and it will be better for you to drive on Saturdays and get to spend some more time with your sons."

I was so grateful for her understanding, but my heart hurt too. I felt guilty and full of regret about spending less time with her and backing away from my original commitment. None of this was easy. Was I making the best decision? Whenever I'd had such tough decisions to make I would have called her for advice, but that wasn't possible anymore and there was no one in my life that could take her place now or in the future — and the loss of her friendship hit me like a ton of bricks. I tried to hide my feelings from her as I continued.

Caring for Mom all week by herself was too much for Isabella. She was exhausted and I had finally convinced her that she needed support. I was going to find someone to help her with the housework and relieve her so she could run errands. So Isabella would be there less, too.

"Does she need help?" Mom asked.

"Yes, Mom, she does," I said. "I think that your insurance will cover it, too."

"I didn't know that she needed help," Mom said. "She hasn't said anything."

The moment I was safely in the car, I started crying and cried most of the drive home. I cried for all of it: my exhaustion, my stress, Isabella's stress, missing Gabriel and Jessie, grieving her impending death and grieving the loss of my best friend.

Chapter Four

Our Daily Angels

Stay open and help will come your way,

and sometimes from complete strangers.

Say yes to any help that is offered,

and if no one offers, ask.

You will be surprised by people's generosity.

None of us can travel this journey alone,

and being able to refuel and take little breaks

will help you stay healthy

and present for your loved one.

Day 67, Saturday, Feb. 19, 2011

I arrived in Santa Maria on a brilliant sunny day to find Isabella greeting me at the door, looking rested and hugging me tight. "I don't know why I resisted having someone help me," she said. "Angelica's a sweetie and takes good care of Mom, and it's a relief to have help with the housework. Thank you, Sis."

Angelica was our new in-home support attendant, coming six days a week to do housework and make breakfast. She had been easy to find with a few phone calls and a little paperwork. Angelica's help allowed Isabella to run errands during the day and catch up on sleep if Mom was up during the night. That was becoming the norm. Isabella would have to stay up with Mom most of the night. We had Angelica for only 24 hours a week, but it made a huge difference. She was turning out to be a godsend.

I walked into the living room and saw Mom sitting in her recliner. "Hello, beautiful Mama. How are you doing?" I said as I brushed her wispy bangs from her forehead and kissed her.

"About the same, Mia. So good to see you. Did you bring me doughnuts?" she said with a big smile.

"Of course! I know that I can't come and visit

you without my friend Krispy Kreme!" I said, smiling back.

"Bring me a lemon-filled bar with a little milk and come sit with me for a while before you start cooking," she said.

This time, Gabriel and Jessie had stayed behind with John, so it was only Sophia and me this weekend.

"I have a surprise for you," I said. I reached into the bag and handed her a beautifully wrapped present.

"My calendar! Oh, thank you, Mia," she said as she took it from me and held it close to her heart. She quickly opened it and started looking through it, slowly passing to view all the pictures of her beloved family. It was a monthly 8 x 10 calendar and every month included various seasonal photos of my family, our beloved mother and her dogs. October was my favorite, with fun photos of Gabriel and Jessie in last year's Halloween costumes. Gabriel had been a Summa Ballerina with a blond Marilyn Monroe wig and Jessie had been a giant shark that ate Justin Bieber. "I love it, Mia. This is the best one you've ever made for me. I love the other 15, but this is my favorite."

"It starts in February. And I'm sorry that it's late..."

"It's perfect, Mia, and with everything you have going on I'm so grateful that you made it," she said.

I hung the calendar next to her bed and opened it to February. The border had tiny hearts for Valentine's Day and there were four photos of all of us smiling and being silly, including little Sophia on the page above the calendar. Mom looked at it, and her smile warmed my heart.

"You know, Mia, I wanted to go to college," she said. "My teachers thought I'd get scholarships, but there was no way I could go. My mom needed me to work in the fields and help support our family. I've loved hearing about all your travels and I feel like I've been to London, Beijing, New York, all the amazing places you've been, Mia. I got to experience the big world with you. I never dreamed you'd travel so much."

"Ah, thank you, Mom," I said. "I had no idea that you wanted to go to college and travel."

"You have such a beautiful way about you, Mia. You have no idea just how beautiful and graceful you are," she said. "I think you need be married to one of our presidents."

"Oh, Mom, you're too much!" I giggled, and then I pondered what her life would have been if she had been able to go to college. "What did you want to study?"

"Business, just like you," she said.

This was the first time we ever talked about her dreams of college and travel. The only dream she'd ever shared with me was how much she wanted to have children. After my father died in 1994, Mom began to travel with two of her nieces, Julia and Angie. They joined a local seniors group and went on numerous trips, including a trip to the Holy Land, and then to Rome, where they toured the Vatican and listened to Pope John Paul II speak during a private appointment with her group. She had been healthy then and able to travel, racking up several trips in ten years.

"What was your favorite trip?" I asked.

"The Holy Land and the Vatican were my favorites. I had goose bumps on the entire trip. And seeing Pope John Paul II speak was magical, Mia."

Her eyes grew big and twinkly. I looked over at

her picture with Pope John Paul II on her wall and felt her love, and wished I'd been there to share it with her.

"I felt the same way about the Vatican. I hope to visit the Holy Land someday, too," I said. "See, you've been somewhere I haven't."

"Weren't you detained by Israeli airport security?" I asked, trying to imagine my dear sweet Mom with large soldiers escorting her to be interrogated.

Mom had traveled to the Holy Land with my cousins Julia and Angie on a trip that took her to Jesus' burial site (The Garden Tomb), Jesus' birth location (the Church of Nativity), where Gabriel told Mary of the Immaculate Conception (Church of the Annunciation). But at the airport on their way home, Mom got singled out for a secondary security check.

"Yes, they took me to a little room and searched me. They had machine guns, Mia, and I was so scared," she said, and I remembered that Julia and Angie were able to get her released in a short time.

"I can't believe that they thought my dear Mama was a security threat," I said.

"I also loved Victoria, B.C.," she continued. "The flowers were so beautiful. I'd never seen or smelled so many gorgeous flowers in one city before. And everyone was so nice."

I had not accompanied her to Victoria, though I had been to the city — but just as quickly, her mind turned to the time she visited me in Alaska, the trip she always called our big adventure on Mount Denali. I was living there, and she and my young nephew came to visit for three weeks.

"I can't believe our plane got stuck in the snow after landing on Mount Denali, right below the crest," she said. "We had to actually get out so the pilot could try and dig us out."

I picked up the story. "You were so excited to be walking on snow for the first time in your life, and I was terrified because our plane was stuck in an ice field with giant crevices. I can't believe that you didn't fall through the snow. I sank up to my hips with every step I took."

We had to walk about a hundred yards across the ice field. And when the pilot got the plane unstuck, he had to take off heading downhill, straight into more ice fields.

"And you were laughing through all of it," I said. "I was terrified."

"It's been a good life, Mia. I'm just not ready to leave all of you." She took my hand.

I wished right then that I had words to console her, but I had none. Instead, I held her hand quietly for a few minutes.

After our chat, she napped. I entered the kitchen, and unloaded my large ice chest. It was filled with all the ingredients that I needed for this weekend's recipes. I was making Mom one of her favorite soups, my Portuguese grandma Amelia's fish stew.

I chopped onions, garlic, red bell peppers, celery, and tomatoes, and sautéed them in a little olive oil. I added tomato sauce and homemade fish stock, white rice, potatoes, fresh lime juice and two whole serrano chiles, red snapper and fresh chopped cilantro. I also made fresh biscuits and Rice Krispy treats for dessert. I checked on Mom and she was still sleeping and I quietly took the dogs out into the backyard. It was cool and sunny and the dogs ran around on the lawn in zigzag patterns chasing each other.

Our playtime was cut short. Her bell was ringing. I ran back inside the house to her side, quickly removing her the mask, as she coughed. She was gagging. I rubbed her back as I watched her struggle to loosen the phlegm from her lungs.

At last she caught a breath. "You made me Grandma's fish soup," she said.

"Yes, but without the fish heads," I said.

"That's how your grandma taught me to make it, and your dad loved it," she said.

"It's a great recipe, but those fish eyes staring back at me from my bowl used to freak me out and even gave me nightmares," I said. "I'd see them sadly asking me why we'd killed them."

"Ay, Mia," she said, laughing.

I brought her soup and biscuits. "The soup is so good. But I think you forgot to put butter on my biscuit," she said.

"Really, Mom, you mean you want more butter."

I took her biscuit and added butter. As we ate together, we chatted about my Portuguese grandparents. My grandma Amelia was a petite sweet woman who had spoiled me rotten. Some of my fondest memories were of her sneaking me into her breakfast nook and having coffee with her so we could catch up. I later learned that it was warm milk with sugar, but I thought I was so grown up, drinking from her beautiful china cups.

After Grandma Amelia died, my Grandpa Alfred lived with us for about four years. I was in first grade when he moved in, and Mom fixed up the spare room in the back of the house for him. He'd meet me at the bus stop every day at the end of our long road and walk me home. He bought me my first bicycle and bought a three-wheel bike for himself so he could ride with me.

Grandpa Alfred was one of the nicest people I've ever known, and Mom had cared for him until he passed away. I found him the morning that he had a terrible stroke. Mom drove him to the hospital, and I sat in the back seat of our Oldsmobile, holding his head. He lasted for a month in the hospital, paralyzed and never able to speak again. I went to see him several times and he would try to speak to me, and just cry out of pure frustration. I was devastated when he died. I wept all the time and was severely depressed for weeks until my dream. I dreamed that he'd visited me. He sat on my bed and told me how much he loved me and that he was okay. He asked me to grow up and make my parents proud, and said he'd always be with me. He put on his hat, kissed my cheek and left. I woke up feeling so much better and told Mom about my dream. She explained that it hadn't been a dream at all. Grandpa had come to visit me.

As we sat there sharing these fond memories, I suddenly remembered that she'd be gone soon. She would no longer be here to talk to, laugh with, taste test, explain and *listen*. I knew that I'd never find anyone ever again with Mom's eagerness to listen to me. No one had her ability to make me feel like she truly heard me.

"I need to check the stove," I said. "I might have left it on."

But that was me, pretending. I needed to run to the kitchen so I could get myself back together as I struggled not to cry in front of her. *Be grateful for now,* I repeated in my mind until I calmed down and returned to the living room to finish eating dinner with her.

"Oh, Mia, I sure hope you made enough soup

for me to share with my hospice nurses," she said when I sat back down across from her. "I've been telling them about your grandmother's Portuguese soups and now they can sample my favorite one."

"Mom, it's me, your daughter — of course I made a huge pot of soup, and I'm delighted that you can share it with your amazing hospice team," I said.

"They're angels, Mia," she said. "My hospice women, Jackie the Rabbi, Sister Beth Ann, the sweet nurses and Angelica. I would have never guessed that I'd have this level of help from strangers at this point in my life. Some are Catholic, Jewish, Jehovah's Witness, and no one is trying to convert me or each other. They all respect each other."

"It's not surprising to me, Mom," I said. "This is how you lived your life. Open, accepting, loving to all. It makes complete sense that you'd be surrounded by an army of people with different backgrounds and beliefs, but all good, wonderful people. It's your karma, Mom, and what you created."

She smiled and said nothing. But I recognized the look: contentment and peace. This amazing woman, my beloved mother and best friend, had found a way to bring contentment and peace into her dying process. I was in complete awe.

Mom knew all about her caregivers' personal lives, their joys, heartbreak and dreams. They adored her. Jackie, the rabbi, had studied in Israel and worked with children. She was in her 60s and had a new boyfriend, and Mom was encouraging her to enjoy her life and pursue her new love. Angelica had two sons in their 20s, and the oldest was about to get married. Her husband had diabetes and had to work out of Santa Maria during the week to support his family. Sister Beth Ann practiced Reiki, and Mom shared very little about her personal life. I didn't ask because I'm sure Mom was honoring her privacy because she was a nun. But I was sure that Mom knew secrets about her life, too.

The hospice nurses continuously said, "We're breaking the rules with your mom, but we love her." They would visit Mom on their days off and often brought her little gifts of cookies and chocolates. Mom was a magnet for love, and I had learned to share her long ago.

When it came time to pack up the car about 4 in the afternoon on Sunday, the little yorkies, Lulu and Gigi escaped from Mom's house and jumped in my car right along with Sophia. They were clearly ready for a ride. It broke my heart to take them back to Mom's house.

As I pulled out of the driveway, I looked back at Mom's front door. Countless times she had stood at the door to wave goodbye. I knew she would never be able to come to the door again. The door to her house was closed, no love pouring out to me, not the way it had been for all of my journeys home for most of my life. I would start this journey without that. The tears rolled down my face.

I got home at 7:30 that night. John was there to greet me with a hug.

"Did something happen?"

Clearly he had noted my swollen eyes.

"More of the same, honey," I said. "I'm grateful for this time I have with her. It was a great visit, but I know that these are borrowed days. She's dying."

I was openly crying. He hugged me and gently kissed my forehead.

John's mother had died 20 years earlier from cancer, just six months after she was diagnosed, and he was incredibly supportive of me spending as much time as I could with my Mom. Gabriel and Jessie had stayed with him over the weekend, and he had helped Jessie with a big school project.

The boys came out of their rooms to greet me and ask about their grandmother. I told them that she was about the same, and Gabriel insisted that she would be better soon. Neither of them spoke about my crying, but I could see that Mom's dying process was taking its toll on them, too.

Jessie showed me a school project he had prepared for Monday's innovation contest. He was going to build the NYC Twin Towers, and he had to assemble the entire project at school during the contest. He and John had drawn out the design and then purchased all the building materials and cut up the wood, and sorted out where to glue it and add brackets. They had built a large base for the entire thing to stand on.

***

Monday morning came, and I called Mom on my way to work. I began to give her an update on Jessie's contest later in the day, but she had to hang up because of a bad coughing spell. This was the norm now. Our phone conversations were usually cut short by one of Mom's alarming coughing spells. I did my best to hold back my tears as I drove the rest of the way to work. *Diana, focus on the fact that she's still here*, I kept telling myself. *You've had 70 days longer than the doctors told you, be grateful!* But my heart ached knowing that my daily phone calls with my best friend were numbered.

At dinner that night, Jessie announced that he won the innovation contest. The Twin Tower design and construction plan that he and John developed worked perfectly, and he was able to build it in the allotted time. I loved seeing him so excited and proud, and Mom was elated when I gave her Jessie's news later in the evening.

Immediately after we spoke, Isabella called, clearly annoyed. "Some doctor is coming later in the week to evaluate Mom. She's been in hospice for so long, and they might need to release her from their services."

I was baffled. "Can they do that?"

Mom was bedridden, unable to walk, had a catheter...

"Yes, they can," she said. "It happens sometimes, and it will mean that Mom will lose most of her support. I can cover her nursing needs, but the big one will be the cost of all her medications, especially her pain pills, and none of us can afford to cover that for her."

I could not get past my shock. "I just can't believe that they think she's well enough not to be in hospice."

"It's not her nurses, Diana," Isabella said. "It's their policy, and they're set up to support patients with less than six months. Mom's near the three-month anniversary."

"When do they come?" I said.

"Later this week," Isabella said. "I told Mom and she was confused. She asked if they thought she was getting better, because she doesn't feel any better. I tried to explain that is more routine than anything else, but I'm not sure she understands the implications if she's released."

"It's probably better that she doesn't understand, Isabella. No need for her to worry about that, too."

I went to work on Thursday morning and could think of nothing else but Mom's hospice evaluation. If they decided to release her, we might have to move her to an extended care facility. And I knew that she desperately wanted to spend her final days in her home.

The doctor was scheduled to arrive between 11 a.m. and noon. At 11:01 a.m. I began checking my phone what felt like every moment for a missed call or text as I sat at my desk. My heart was pounding loudly when my phone rang at 12:05 p.m. Isabella called me the moment he left.

"He didn't release her," she said. "She is far too ill. He's rather surprised she's holding on."

"Oh, thank goodness," I said, feeling so relieved knowing that I could continue to visit and cook for her. "Did he have an update on how long we have, Sis?"

"No, I don't think he wanted to touch it after the whole 'three days to live' thing."

Day 82, Sat., March 5, 2011

"Hello beautiful Mom," I said as we entered the living room with John and, of course, little Sophia.

"You made good time today, Mia." Mom said as she looked up at me while I kissed her forehead.

She was sitting in her recliner and looked happy and excited. Today was Renee's baby shower, which meant the scheduled arrival of her first great-granddaughter was only a few weeks away.

"Isabella is already at the hall, decorating. Angelica is going to stay with me. Just bring us some food from the party," Mom instructed.

Then, she added with a twinkle in her eyes. "Of course, if I get too hungry, Angelica can give me one of the Krispy Kremes you snuck into the kitchen."

"Of course we brought you doughnuts, and have one if you like," I said. "I won't tell Isabella."

"I'm proud of you, Mia, for not volunteering to cook today," Mom said. "I knew you wanted to."

"It was really hard for me not to offer to make the beans, rice, salsa, and guacamole, Mom, but I knew I just couldn't manage right now," I said.

"Make sure you bring me some cake," Mom said.

My cousin Maria was bringing a pink champagne cake (white cake with Bavarian and whipped cream filling) from the Madonna Inn, just as she had for my son Gabriel's baby shower.

"It's the best," she said.

"I'll try to make it home with your cake, but I'll have to hide it from John," I said. "You know how he is about cake."

She turned to my man. "John, you better not eat all my cake," she said jokingly.

As we left a few minutes later, I was amazed at Mom's ability to be cheerful today. I knew that she would have loved to go to her eldest granddaughter's baby shower, but her poor health prohibited it.

John dropped me off at the shower a few minutes later. This was a traditional female-family-only event. When I entered the little community hall I smelled the oak wood burning in the barbecue pit. It ushered in a flood of memories of family parties held over the years, all with Mom and her cooking at the center of every single one.

I visited with several cousins and old friends, and we had a delightful afternoon. A few asked about Mom's condition, but I was grateful that everyone's primary focus was the upcoming birth of Renee's baby girl. We played a few games and ate a traditional Santa Maria-style barbecue menu: grilled chicken, chili beans, green salad, potato salad and grilled buttered French bread with yummy salsa. Renee's dad grilled the chicken and bread, and various family members made all the other side dishes. This was the first family party I'd attended where Mom hadn't made the chili beans, rice and potato salad and I hadn't made the salsa.

Renee and Christina didn't mention their grandmother Rose during the entire party. My mother had been a big part of their lives and cared for them after school while their mother, Isabella, was working. My nieces adored their grandmother and like me had fond memories of her being healthier, cooking all the time, traveling, going to their various sporting and school events — and today, on the biggest event of either of their lives, she and her delicious food were absent.

John and I returned to Mom with dinner and cake after the baby shower. She listened intensely and ate a little bit of her dinner as Isabella and I shared all the events from the party, including a little family gossip. Later Renee came over to visit and proudly showed her grandmother all her gifts. Mom was sitting in her recliner, and Renee sat in a chair next to her with her enormous baby belly popping out in front of her. Mom was beaming as she examined about 50 outfits in bright colors: pink, yellow, purple, green dresses, onesies, overalls, pajamas, with flowers, animal prints and fun patterns. There were also several cute rattles, baby mobiles, stuffed animals and homemade blankets. "Oh, Mia, you got so many nice things," Mom said to Renee.

"I know, Grandma," replied Renee with a big lingering smile.

As I watched, I found it hard not to be sad. Mom would never go to any of her great-granddaughter's birthday parties, her baptism, her first soccer game — and yet she was happy. My heart literally hurt, knowing that Marisol would have none of these memories with her sweet great-grandmother, and I struggled to hold back my tears. And I quietly prayed to the Blessed Virgen. *Oh, please just let her get to hold this baby.* I was prepared to bargain just about anything including shortening my life span so that my sweet mama could have this last wish.

The next morning when I removed Mom's mask, I struggled to rewire her oxygen. The open sores around the edges of the mask oozed, and I felt intimidated about my ability to do this right as I saw her grimace.

"I'm so sorry, Mom," I said.

"It hurts, Mia," she said. "Isabella and the nurses keep trying to figure something out, but nothing seems to work."

I knew that Isabella has asked around to everyone and continued to research options on the Internet. "I can't even begin to comprehend how much it must hurt." I sadly looked at her, wishing for a magic wand.

I looked at the small table next to the recliner and hospital bed, and was struck that the table was filled with figurines of angels. I quickly thanked them for helping to keep Mom alive, and asked if they could somehow reduce her pain too.

"I smell garlic, Mia. What are you cooking?" I heard her words but I also saw the sadness and pain in her eyes.

"I'm making you Grandma Amelia's clam chowder," I said. "I thought you might like fresh soup for the week."

"Oh, Mia, you didn't need to cook me anything

today. There is so much barbecue left over from Renee's baby shower," she said, "but I do love your grandma's clam chowder."

There, she gave me a small smile. But she refused to have any breakfast except for her banana, coffee, juice and her pills. I continued to be amazed that she was able to keep all her medication straight as I watched her carefully sort out her morning med cocktail.

In the kitchen, I finished sautéing the chopped onions, celery and garlic. I mixed in the clams, fish stock and potatoes and let it all simmer for about 30 minutes, stirring in heavy cream last.

Mom's appetite was worsening, and she had lost more weight. I knew I needed to get more creative with my cooking if there was any hope of her eating.

"Do you want to taste the soup?" I asked as she woke up from her morning nap.

"Oh, yes, please," she said with big eyes.

I sat beside her hospital bed with a spoonful of clam chowder and fed her. "Does it need anything?"

"No, Mia, it's perfect and I like the changes you made to my recipe. Did you use cream instead of milk?"

"Yes, master chef. You busted me. Are you sure it doesn't need salt?"

"It doesn't need anything," she said. "It's delicious. Can you bring me a little bowl with some bread?"

Later, as the day warmed I took Gigi, Lulu and Sophia for their Sunday walk to the school and let them run. Alone at the school park, I tried to remind myself that she had only a few more weeks left before she'd meet her great granddaughter, but then what...? Would she die the day after? I kept trying to quiet my mind and just be grateful that she'd exceeded her prognosis by more than 70 days. No matter how hard I tried to bring my focus back to the dogs, who were immensely enjoying their walk, my heart sank. I could not imagine a life without my sweet mama around to listen to me, cheer me on and be my daily champion. My best friend was on borrowed time.

Marisol would be born in just a few weeks, a milestone I thought we would never have reached with my mother still in our lives.

Day 89, Saturday, March 12, 2011

I had bonded with Highway 101. By this point, I knew where all the clean bathrooms were, the places for Sophia to walk, the safest gas stations. I was a living Yelp review for the whole route between Redwood City and Santa Maria.

It had been a tough week. Gabriel and Jessie were busy with school, tutoring, music, basketball, and I was in the middle of one of the most challenging projects of my entire career at my global high-tech company. I was leading the redesign of our 42 country websites, and the deadlines were very aggressive.

Mom's ability to speak to me on the phone continued to decline. Her coughing attacks, gasping for air, weakness were all contributing factors that made communicating with me almost impossible. But if I didn't call every evening, she worried. It broke my heart to put her through the paces of trying to speak to me.

This time when I arrived, she was watching the Lakers game. "I was worried about you, Mia," she said. "It's late. Did you hit bad traffic?"

"Just a little," I said. "I went to the grocery store

this morning. I'm going to make you chicken mole and I needed to get all the chiles. No lazy mole with chile powder for my Mama."

"Oh, Mia, that's so much work," she said. "I worry about you coming every weekend, working all week, taking care of your family. You're not resting. You have huge circles under your eyes."

"Please don't worry about me," I said, feeling awful that she had noticed I was tired. Her ability to show compassion for me even now, as she fought for every breath, astonished me. And I didn't think it was good for her to worry. She needed every ounce of her energy to keep her alive long enough to meet Marisol.

"I have a big surprise for you, Mom. Jessie finished scanning all your pictures. He scanned almost 1,400 photos. And now that I have them all in digital format, I'm going to make DVDs for everyone in our family so no one will be fighting over which photos they got or didn't get."

She thanked me, then she said, "I don't even think I understand what you mean by scanning."

I explained that scanning was taking a high-quality picture of a printed picture and turning it into a digital image so you can see it on your computer, use it in home movies, make reprints, etc. "Jessie was so cute," I said. "He asked what was wrong with the first black-and-white photo. He'd never seen one before."

When we sat down later to look at all the photos, Mom was thrilled to see them. Her eyes were huge with joy as she shared various stories about her lifetime memories. She didn't notice that I had tears in my eyes the whole time.

I had edited several of the black and white photos and improved their quality. I tried to focus on how happy it made Mom to see all her pictures on my laptop. The circle of life was remarkable. There were adorable baby photos of Renee, as a young girl and now she was about to become a mother. "I love that you did this for me, Mia," she said as she took my hand lovingly. I looked down at our hands, and prayed that I'd have a photo to add in a few days of Mom, Renee and Marisol.

Mom returned to her Lakers game on TV, and I went to the kitchen to recreate Mom's famous chicken mole.

So many times I'd made mole with my mother. I knew there were shortcuts to simplify the dish. But not today. I was making it all from scratch. I started boiling the chicken breasts with garlic and onions. In another pot, I started rehydrating the four types of dried chiles with onions and garlic. While they were cooking, I made Mom fresh guacamole and salsa.

"Have you had any lunch yet?" I asked during a commercial break.

"No, Mia. Angelica tried to make me eat something, but I wasn't hungry yet," she said like a small child.

"I made some fresh guacamole and salsa. Do you want some with chips while you watch the game? Or some fresh nachos?"

"Oh, Mia, I was wondering what you were up to. I could smell the fresh cilantro. It smells so good. Make me some nachos, but just a little."

I returned a few minutes later with a plate of nachos — melted cheese, topped with Peruvian beans, guacamole, salsa and a little sour cream.

"Oh, Mia, that's way too much," she said as I placed the plate of nachos on her coffee tray. "You have to help me eat these."

"Sorry, I have mole to make and I don't like sour cream," I said. "Just eat what you can."

"But it's way too much, and it's a sin to waste food," she said, just as she had a million times before and most likely the reason I felt severe guilt for not eating every morsel on my plate.

"Do your best, Mom," I said. "It's really not that much."

She shook her head at me but she started eating the nachos. I checked on her a few times, and a half-hour later the plate was empty.

"I'm so full, Mia, but they were so good," she said.

"I knew you could eat it all, Mom."

The Lakers won. She had a quick telephone conversation with my cousin Maria to rehash the game highlights. I loved that they were sports junkies. I put the mask on her, she took an afternoon nap and I returned to my mole.

I found Mom's cast-iron skillet and started making the roux, the base for my mole and one of the toughest parts of the recipe. When my mama made mole, she made *mole rojo*. And did not add chocolate or pumpkin seeds, like most recipes. She always called it real mole, which let the spicy red chiles take center stage in the dish.

While the olive oil heated up in the cast iron skillet I prepared my chiles. I'd placed them in a food processor, with garlic, onions and a little water, and pureed them. I poured the pureed chile mixture into a large strainer to remove the seeds, and what was left was mole magic.

The next 15 minutes were critical, so I checked on Mom and thankfully she was sleeping. I added flour to the hot oil and began to stir them together rigorously to create a thick roux. When it was golden brown and smooth, I added the chile puree. The roux bubbled as I added the chicken broth and created the lovely rich, thick, dark-red sauce. I left it to simmer for a few minutes. I added salt, ground cloves and the shredded chicken. I knew the ingredients were right, but I needed Mom's taste buds to help me get the flavor just right. Then I made her orange rice. The only thing missing from our feast was Mom's homemade flour tortillas, which I had not learned to make.

Ring, ring, ring! Mom rang her bell, just as I turned off the burner on the rice.

"Did you have a nice nap?" I asked as I started to remove the mask and rewire her oxygen.

"Oh, Mia, the mole smells amazing. It reminds me of when I was a little girl and how our house smelled when my mother made it. Her mole was the best!"

I adjusted her pillows and raised the bed. "It's all done. Do you want to taste it?"

She nodded yes, and I returned with a spoonful of mole.

"It's delicious," she said. "It needs a little more salt, more cloves and even a little more chiles." This was said in her master chef voice.

We kept up this taste-testing ritual for 15 minutes, with me perfecting the dish with a little of that, a little of this, until I received final approval.

"Now it's perfect, Mia," she said.

Hundreds of times we had cooked mole together in her kitchen. There had been parties and holidays and birthdays. We made the mole for tamales. We made the mole for crunchy pork. How was I going to do this?

During dinner, Mom ate every bite and kept thanking me for making her beloved mole. I assured her that I made tons, as I knew she'd want to share some with her hospice team and Angelica.

"I've told everyone about my mole," she said. "None of them have ever had our *mole rojo* without the chocolate and the pumpkin seeds. I can't wait for them to try it, and then they will know just how yummy real mole is."

"I've tried the chocolate stuff, Mom, but I'm not a fan," I said. "I can honestly say that you've ruined me when it comes to mole."

That Sunday, as I left, I had to tell Mom I wouldn't be able to visit the following weekend. John and I were going to take Gabriel and Jessie to Tahoe on a mini-vacation for spring break. She said that would be good for all of us, but I felt guilty and my heart was torn between spending these last days with my mother and spending time with my sons and John.

At Tahoe, we had a wonderful time. Gabriel and Jessie had a blast sledding. We needed this time. On Friday, Gabriel learned he'd been accepted into an all-boy college prep high school that's very selective. He was thrilled and threw himself in the snow.

When I called Mom later to share Gabriel's big news, I knew she was proud of her grandson, but she sounded weak. It was a struggle for her to chat very long.

Day 99, Tuesday, March 22, 2011

Tuesday night, back in Redwood City, my phone buzzed. I was washing dishes, so I turned off the water and dried my hands. I saw I'd received a text. From Isabella.

Renee is in labor.

Tears of joy ran down my face. Mom was still with us, and Mom was going to meet her great-granddaughter.

Chapter Five

Meet Marisol

Your loved one's behavior may

change to the point that you might

not even recognize her.

She may say or do things that are

completely out of character.

If you notice these behavioral changes,

notify your medical professional immediately.

She may be depressed and

suffering from anxiety.

Try to not take selfish behavior personally,

as she is merely trying

to hold on to life for one more day.

Day 101, Thurs., March 24, 2011

I couldn't wait for the weekend to meet little Marisol. My phone was full of adorable photos of Isabella's first granddaughter and Mom's first great-granddaughter. As soon as she was released from the hospital, Renee took Marisol over to meet her great-grandmother. What I wouldn't have given to see that moment when Mom finally met Marisol. I called Mom later to get the update on the grand event.

"Oh, Mia, she's so beautiful. She has so much hair. It's jet black and thick," she said. "And she's so alert. She's already looking at everything and everyone."

Mom continued to fill me on Marisol's birth details, how she smelled, the shape of her hands. My mind raced. Marisol was here, yay! Marisol was here, oh no! Was Mom dying later today, tonight, tomorrow?

As she spoke, I saw my beautiful mama holding Gabriel and Jessie when they were newborns. Her face was filled with love, joy and pride as she held them tightly and examined her grandsons' tiny faces, hands and toes. She continued to share stories about Marisol, and my mind raced with more memories of her with Gabriel and Jessie. I saw her at their baptisms, birthday parties, holidays, sitting on our couch between Gabriel (age 4) and Jessie (age 2), giggling with delight while she tickled them. There would be no photos of Mom and Marisol at age 2 or 4.

My visit down memory lane ended as Mom's excitement triggered a terrible coughing attack. She tried to apologize as she ended our call.

***

Loud noises erupted from the backyard. I opened the kitchen window to peer outside.

"Daddy, what are you doing?"

My father was standing in my mother's backyard.

"We're having a huge party for your mom. Everyone's coming. We can't wait to see her."

He was smiling, standing in front of two wood-burning barbecue grills. Corn on the cob sizzled on one grill, and the fire had kicked up on the second one.

"Is she coming home today?" I asked.

"No, Diana, today's Friday, and she's not coming home until Thursday," he said.

Suddenly, I felt myself in a strong warm embrace. "Babe, Babe, wake up! You're dreaming," John said.

I was crying hysterically. "I had the most realistic dream. My dad was in Mom's backyard, barbecuing for Mom's welcome home party. He told me that she's dying on Thursday."

"It was just a dream, Babe," he said.

John reminded me it was Saturday and I was going to see my sweet mama today. And meet Marisol.

After I was dressed, I parted the blinds in our bedroom to let the sun in. I took a deep breath to calm myself and looked out on our patio. Under the tree I saw an ear of corn.

"John! John!"

I ran to him with tears streaming down my face. I beckoned him to come back to our room. I slid open the glass door and stepped onto the patio, and John followed me.

"Look, there it is!" I said.

I felt my eyes grow huge. I was filled with tears and confusion. A giant ear of corn lay in the dirt. It was stripped to the cob, kernels eaten away. The leaves were pulled back and still attached to the husk.

"Please don't tell me you think your dad left the corn in our backyard," John said.

"I don't know what to think," I said. "But I've never seen any corn lying around in our backyard before. Where did it come from?"

"Babe, a squirrel probably brought it into the yard," he said, trying to squash my ghost story.

"Honey, how could a squirrel carry that? It's huge, and it's not even corn season," I said. "None of our neighbors grow corn in their backyards."

"The squirrel probably got it out of a trash can and brought it up to the tree and dropped it," he said.

"What? No way. I don't know how it got here, but it sure is crazy that my dad was barbecuing corn in my dream, and here it is in our backyard."

John continued to try to convince me that there was some logical explanation of how a corn cob managed to find its way into our backyard, but no matter what he said I knew it was my dad.

All the way to Santa Maria, I couldn't stop thinking about that dream. Growing up, my dad told us frequent stories of visions and dreams about loved ones saying goodbye the night before they died. Sometimes he would have a feeling that someone was going to die, and his premonitions were always right. Was he trying to tell me that this was Mom's last week?

I was an emotional wreck the whole drive. I kept trying to remind myself that I was delighted Marisol had arrived, but the concern about what this meant for Mom's remaining time was stronger.

"Hello, beautiful Great-Grandma," I said as I walked into Mom's living room. I bent down to kiss her on her forehead. She was sitting in her chair, proudly holding Marisol and feeding her with a tiny bottle.

"Hello, Mia. Isn't she gorgeous? And she's such a good eater," Mom said.

"Yes, she is. Just like her great-grandma," I said.

Marisol was neatly swaddled in a pink blanket, wearing a matching beanie. Mom was glowing. She looked peaceful, happy and healthy. Clearly, Daddy's prediction was wrong. There was no way she was dying in five days. This was the best she'd looked in months.

Renee had moved into Mom's house so

Isabella could help her with the baby for a few weeks, and Mom was delighted with this development. Mom clearly knew how to find joy in living in the moment. There was no sadness, regret or feeling sorry for herself that she wasn't going to see Marisol grow up. She was reveling in this moment, this victory of meeting her first great-granddaughter.

As I watched her holding Marisol, images of seeing her hold Gabriel, Jessie, Renee and so many other family and friends' newborns flashed before me. Mom knew her way with babies, and oh how she loved to cook for them. Gabriel and Jessie weighed over 11 pounds when they were born. I wasn't able to breastfeed them due to my hormone inefficiencies. Mom helped me get them started on a regimen of cereal and applesauce when they were just two weeks old to fill their tummies and help them sleep through the night. We had a special bottle for this super baby recipe with the nipple large enough for the applesauce-cereal milkshake to get through. It was genius, and because of her I had newborns who slept through the night. When I tried to tell her that the doctors, parenting books, etc. didn't think this was a good idea, she let me know that she'd done the same with all of us, Isabella's daughters, etc. And all of us had been healthy children, albeit chubby.

She knew how to feed and care for baby animals, too. Growing up on the farm, we raised rabbits for extra money. We often lost a mama rabbit, and if her babies were tiny, Mom would bring them into the house and house them in our oven so the pilot light could keep them warm. She fed them several times a day with an eyedropper until they were big enough to return to their hutches. Mom did the same with newborn calves. We had a special pen for the orphaned calves, and Mom fed them with giant bottles until they were strong enough to return to the calf pens. My mom's DNA had strands that drove her to feed everyone and everything. It was who she was. And now that she was too ill to cook, unable to walk, little Marisol would be the last living creature that she'd ever have the joy of feeding. I know that I inherited some of Mom's food-pusher DNA, too.

"Do you want to hold her?" Mom said as she looked up at me, breaking her gaze from angelic Marisol for a moment.

"Do you need to take a break?" I said.

"No, I'm just trying to share. She doesn't stay

awake too long right now," she said.

"Thanks, Mom, I can hold her later," I said. "You look so good together, and I'm happy to sit here and watch."

Mom gently burped Marisol, and the baby contently fell asleep in Mom's lap. Renee came in to take her but decided to let her sleep. The picture of them together was priceless, and I was so grateful for this moment.

Mom started coughing a few minutes later, and we were all shocked back into reality. Renee quickly took Marisol, and I helped Mom while she struggled to catch her breath. She was slumped over in her chair, and I rubbed her back, trying desperately to help her get the phlegm out.

"I'm tired, Mia, I think I need to take a nap. I'm sorry we didn't get to catch up," she said as she looked up at me.

The joy and contentment drained from her face, replaced with fatigue and discomfort.

"Mom, it's okay," I said. "I loved seeing you with Marisol. We'll talk later. Nothing too exciting going on in my life these days."

"Can you bring me half a lemon doughnut

before I go to sleep?" she said, smiling. "It will help me sleep better. I know you snuck them into the kitchen."

While Mom slept, I began our celebratory feast. I was making *carne de res Milanesa* tacos, one of Mom's favorites.

First, I prepared the breading for the *carne asada* (flat steaks). I'd altered Mom's original recipe and used breadcrumbs, cornmeal, flour, various seasonings and a little ground chipotle chile pepper. I set the breading aside to rest and began to prepare the Peruvian beans. I fried them with bacon, onion flakes, salt, jalapeños and mashed them until they were creamy.

From the other room, Mom rang her bell and I came to remove her mask.

"Oh, Mia, your cooking. The rice and beans smell so good. What else are you making?"

"I'm making *Milanesa* tacos. The guacamole and salsa are ready, too. I just need to fry the *Milanesa*. Are you ready for a dinner?"

"Oh, Mia, that sounds so good. I haven't had them for so long."

The *Milanesa* fried quickly. I chopped it into

cubes, placed it in warm corn tortillas and topped it with guacamole, salsa, onion, cilantro and crema.

"Here you go, Mom, two tacos, a little rice and beans." I placed her plate on her tray.

"Oh, Mia, that looks so good, but it's way too much food," she said as she touched her stomach with her right hand.

"Just eat what you can, Mom," I said.

Isabella, Renee and I made our plates and joined her in the living room.

"The *Milanesa* is delicious, Mia, but it's not my recipe," Mom said. "It's spicier and has corn meal. What did you put in it?"

"Yup, I added a little cornmeal and chipotle chile," I said. "Just trying to keep you on your toes, Mom, and spice up an old favorite."

"It's very, very good. You're such a good cook, Mia. I'm sorry I can't eat anymore. Please save my second taco for tomorrow." She pushed her plate away.

I was disappointed to see how little she ate. "Mom, you have to try and eat more. You're getting too thin. We're going to open the sliding glass door one of these days and the wind is going to blow you out of your bed."

"Ay, si," she said, smiling. That was one of Mom's favorite sayings when she thought anyone was too thin; the wind will blow them over.

I took her half-eaten plate to the kitchen and returned to the living room, where Marisol was awake and hungry.

"Do you want to feed her again, Grandma?" Renee said.

"No, Mia, I think it's your Aunt Diana's turn," she said.

Renee handed me the baby, and I sat on the couch and fed her. Mom watched from her hospital bed, but she wasn't there with us in the room. Was she thinking about how much time she had left, now that her prayers had been answered and she'd met Marisol?

Marisol finished her bottle and was comfortably lying in my lap, looking around the room. Her big alert brown eyes looked everywhere. Sophia stretched her front paws out on my legs and tried to get a closer look at Marisol. "She won't hurt her," I said as I saw Renee's concerned look. "She just wants to see your beautiful little girl."

"Gigi and Lulu have been trying to smell her all week," Renee said.

"I wonder if they know that she's your daughter," I said, scratching Sophia's little ears.

"Of course they do," Mom said. "Don't you remember how your dad tied the hide of a stillborn calf around a live orphan newborn calf so the grieving mama cow would nurse it?"

"I'd forgotten all about that, Mom," I said. "How many calves did he save that way?"

"Oh, so many, Mia. It saved the mamas, too, because they needed to be milked after their calves were born. And they would cry when their calves were dead."

"Really, Grandma, cows can cry?" Renee said.

"Yes, they'd moan and moo for hours," Mom said. "It was heartbreaking to hear. And they would try licking and pushing their newborn calves to stand or move. It was so sad to watch."

"I remember trying to help Daddy with birthing cows whose calves got stuck," I said. "We'd pull the calves out with a winch that was attached to the front of one of the ranch trucks."

Renee's eyes got big.

"He'd tie the cable to their hooves, and we'd gently pull them out. Sometimes they were already dead, or died instantly, and we lost several mamas, too," I said.

"That sounds so gross," Renee said finally.

"Oh, Renee, you guys are so spoiled, never dealing with where your food comes from." Mom shook her head.

"The worst was when the cows got out at night," I said. "Daddy would wake us up and we'd get buckets of oats and flashlights, and out we'd go into the dark, scary ranch all in different directions to find the cows and lure them back to their corrals. This always happened when it was raining and the wind was blowing. I was terrified."

"You were such a big chicken," Mom said, smiling.

"Really, Mom, it was terrifying," I said.

"Grandma, there's no way that I would do that," Renee said. "Chase cows in the dark."

"Daddy worked so hard," I said, looking at Mom.

"Yes, he did. Rain or shine, he was working, milking cows, helping them give birth, washing the barns, 16-hour days and only five days off a month," Mom said.

My father had been dead for almost 17 years. Mom had never removed his name from her bank account checks, and lots of clothes were still in one of the closets, but she rarely spoke about him—so it was highly unusual for her to reminisce about him for so long. I thought about telling her about my dream and decided not to. "Mia, can I have the second half of my doughnut?"

"Ay, Mama, you didn't eat your dinner because you were too full, but you have room for more doughnut," I said.

I returned with her Krispy Kreme lemon-filled doughnut and a small glass of milk. "I need you to drink all your milk, too."

"I love these doughnuts so much. Thank you, Mia."

I could see that Isabella started to say something about Mom's doughnut addiction and then decided not to. How could we be mad at her for something that gave her so much pleasure?

Renee went to bed early and took little Marisol with her.

"She's a good mother, Mia," Mom said proudly after Renee left the room.

"Well, look at who her grandma is."

***

The television was off, and Isabella and I reminisced with Mom for hours about our mishaps and adventures on the dairy farm. Mom was engaged and enjoyed our slight exaggerations about visits to our relatives and her rules.

"Do you remember making us go visit our Aunt Mary and Uncle John?" I said. "They didn't have electricity or running water, and lived out on a farm in the middle of nowhere. And she never combed her hair, her white wiry hair. I swear she looked like a witch. We'd try to get Daddy out of there quickly, but it never worked. Eventually we'd have to go to the bathroom, an outhouse with magazines for toilet paper, and we'd always be leaving in the dark, and then I'd have to get out of the car and open the gate at the end of the road for Daddy. It's no wonder I have nightmares."

"Ay, Mia, they were really nice people," Mom said.

"What, I don't remember them," Isabella said.

"You were too young, and you're lucky you don't remember," I said. "And I know you'd agree that she looked like the old witch with the poison apple in *Snow White*."

Mom laughed. "You always did have a vivid imagination."

We moved from scariest family visits into worst food experiences without skipping a beat. Our mother's cooking had turned us into foodie snobs at very young ages. Thankfully most of our relatives were great cooks, and eating in their homes was a delight. Mom was clear about the rules of dining in others' homes; we were always expected to try all the dishes, eat every morsel on our plates, help clean up and thank our relatives for our wonderful meal.

Unfortunately, my dad's brother and his wife missed the good food gene. They were two of the nicest people on the planet, but eating in their homes was a scary experience. We were usually successful in getting my father to end our visit before mealtimes, but one Sunday afternoon our good fortune ran out.

"Oh, Mom, do you remember that liver and gravy dinner with Uncle Frank and Aunt Beatrice?" I

said.

"Oh, Mia, how could I ever forget it," she said, her eyes widening.

"It was the worst," Isabella said, joining in the story.

"We all sat at their table, and Aunt Beatrice's dentures were in a glass by the sink right next to the kitchen table. I remember looking at you, Mom, and trying to send you a telepathic message to come up with some excuse as to why we couldn't eat dinner. I saw the large bowl of fried liver with white gravy placed on the table, and there was blood oozing out of the uncooked liver. As much as I tried to signal you, you said nothing. And then, their kids started putting their dirty little hands right into the bowl and removing the pieces of liver. And then you finally saved us."

"Yes, I did," Mom said. "The undercooked liver and the hands were too much for me, and I made some excuse about you kids being full or something. I felt terrible for lying."

"Mom, from the bottom of my heart, thank you for lying. I will never forget that food, and boy, was I glad you broke your rules and saved us."

Mom was shaking her head, still in disbelief

that someone would undercook liver and serve it with a white gravy. "I've never been a fan of white gravy," she said. "There's just not any flavor."

We spoke for some time about our uncle, his wife and other relatives who had died, fond memories and how much we missed all of them. My sweet mama had outlived all her six siblings, and all our grandparents were gone, as were all but one of my dad's five siblings.

Somehow Isabella and I started whispering about Mom's gifts, and her greatest gift ever.

"What are you two talking about?" Mom said.

"Well, Mom, we wanted you to know what we think the greatest gift is that you ever gave us. Isabella and I are fairly sure that it's the same for both of us even though we've never spoken about it," I said proudly.

"Really?" Mom said, tilting her head and placing her hand underneath her chin, her signal to go on and that she was intently listening.

"You taught us not to hate people based on the color of their skin," I said. "You were made to sit at the back of the bus, drink from non-white water fountains, go to the movies on non-whites-only nights and other horrible segregation and mistreatment as a young woman, and yet you never told us anything about any of it until we were all grown up and we asked you about it."

Isabella nodded in agreement, and Mom said nothing.

"I was about 25 when I asked you about why you never told us any of these stories while we were growing up," I said. "You said that you wanted the hate to end with me." Tears came to my eyes.

"I didn't want you girls to hate anyone because of what had happened to me," Mom said. "I didn't want you judge people because of the color of their skin. I knew how much that hurt, and I never wanted my children to treat anyone poorly because of my life experiences."

"We were so lucky that you had that foresight, Mom," I said. "To understand that sharing those stories with us would have made us prejudiced, and instead you hid it from us so we could see people and not colors. This is a remarkable gift, Mom."

I could see Mom was touched, but far too humble to think that she could have kept at least two people from being prejudiced. But she had.

Sunday morning, I woke up early and started cooking Mom's beef vegetable soup, *caldo de res*. I carefully washed the beef short ribs. Then I cut up a large onion, celery and crushed garlic cloves in the *molcajete*. I placed the short ribs and all the other items in a large soup pan and let the magic begin. I sautéed everything and browned the short ribs. I added water, lowered the heat and let the stock slowly simmer.

"Good morning, beautiful Mama," I said as I started to remove the mask.

"You're making me *caldo de res*. It smells so good, Mia," she said. "But why did you get up so early to cook? You need to rest, and there are leftovers from last night's feast and..."

"It's cold outside, and I wanted you to have some fresh soup for the week," I said. "I'm happy to make it for you, Mom, and I know you'd be doing the same for me if our situation was reversed."

"You and Isabella are the best daughters ever," she said sadly.

I looked at her closely, her thin weak body, immobile and struggling to breathe, and yet she was worried about me getting up early. That was Mom.

We chatted for a little while longer, and she had a horrible coughing spell. "I'm going to wake up Marisol," she said sadly in between coughs.

"It's okay, Mom," I said. "It's good for Marisol to get used to noise, and even better if she can sleep through it."

The coughing subsided after about five minutes, and I gave her cranberry juice and a banana and she took her morning meds. She was quiet and started watching Sunday Mass on her TV. I returned to kitchen to finish our *caldito*. I cut up fresh tomatoes, added a couple of jalapeños, diced potatoes, peeled fresh corn and sliced cabbage.

I returned to living room and watched the end of Mass with Mom. She responded out loud to the participatory parts of the Mass, and I prayed with her. She had her rosary beads on her tray, and I was sure that she was thanking God, the Virgen de Guadalupe, saints, angels and a host of spirits for allowing her to live long enough to meet little Marisol.

I added in the final ingredients, carrots and zucchini, to my *caldo de res* and took the dogs for a walk. Sophia, Lulu and Gigi made our weekly visit to the nearby school so they could run through the thick grass. When I returned from our walk, the soup was ready.

"Mom, I tried the soup, but it's missing something," I said. "Can you help me?"

"It smells so good, Mia," she said. "I can't wait to taste it."

"It's still a little hot," I said as I fed her a spoonful of the broth.

"Oh, Mia, it's delicious," she said. "It needs a tiny bit of cloves. Are you going to serve it with a little fresh cilantro, fresh squeezed lime juice and avocado?" I welcomed her master chef persona.

"Yes, Mom," I said. "You taught me well, and that makes it so yummy. I forgot to get us fresh French bread, so I'm baking cornbread too."

"You're spoiling me," Mom said.

"Yes I am, and I love it." I bent down and kissed her forehead.

A few minutes later I returned with a plate of *caldo de res* and fresh cornbread soaked in butter.

"I won't be able to eat all of that," Mom said when she saw the bowl.

"Eat what you can, Mom," I said. "Hopefully

you won't be returning the cornbread for more butter."

She looked up at me smiling and shook her head gently as she saw the butter spilling out of the cornbread. I sat on the sofa and ate with her. Isabella and Renee were both taking a nap, and it was nice to visit with Mom for a few minutes before I started driving home. I updated her on Gabriel and Jessie, my work and John.

"Marisol is so adorable, Mom," I finally said. "It was so great to see you hold her."

"Yes, Mia, it is so nice to finally meet her," Mom said sadly.

Her great joy from the day before was gone, and there was a knowing that her miracle had been granted and her exit was closer. I said nothing and sat with her. She finished her lunch and quietly looked out the window. I could feel her sadness and quietly held her hand.

I returned to the kitchen, washed our dishes and finished packing my car. I said goodbye to Marisol, Renee, Isabella, little Lulu and Gigi. I blessed Mom's forehead in the sign of the cross and kissed her goodbye. I rushed out of the house before anyone could see the tears on my face. I cried most of the way home. My mind raced with worry about Mom's remaining time. I tried to be grateful for the last four months, but it was no use. Nothing worked, and the tears just kept rolling. I didn't know what to pray for now.

Day 107, Wednesday, March 30, 2011

The next week went by quickly. My daily phone calls with Mom were more challenging than ever. Our calls seemed to stimulate a coughing attack, and our conversations were lasting less than two minutes. I was conflicted about calling her. I didn't want her to worry about me, and I didn't want to be the reason that she couldn't breathe. On Wednesday, I decided that maybe it was time to let go of our daily phone call ritual and didn't call her.

"I was worried, are you OK? It's after 9 p.m. and you hadn't called yet." Mom said as I answered the phone.

"I'm fine, Mom, I was just busy with Gabriel and Jessie and thought it might be too late to call you," I

said.

"I don't care what time it is, Mia, you need to call me or I worry," she said.

"Sorry, Mom, and I promise I will call you. I don't want you to worry."

Day 117, Sat., April 9, 2011

Mom didn't want Isabella to leave her alone for even a moment. She was depressed and crying frequently.

"I don't even recognize her anymore, Diana," Isabella said. "She's so demanding and clingy. She doesn't even want me to take a shower."

Isabella was briefing me during a phone call as John and I drove to Santa Maria.

"This isn't our Mom, Isabella," I said. "She's struggling to live. Our Mom would never behave like this. You must know that. Now that Marisol has arrived, I'm sure she thinks her time has run out."

"But you're not here with her every day," Isabella said. "It's so hard to see."

I heard the tears in her voice. "I will talk to her, Sis. I wish I could be there more." And then I had another thought. "Has she started taking her new antidepressants and anti-anxiety medicines?" I could never stop feeling guilty about the brunt of Mom's care falling to Isabella.

"Yes, but it will take a couple of weeks for the medicine to start working," she said.

When we arrived at Mom's on Easter weekend, I announced no cooking tonight. "John is going to pick us up dinner from Shaw's," I said. "I'm craving their yummy steaks."

"I can't eat very much, Mia. Just get me the smallest little thing," she said.

"Don't worry, Mom," I said, "We'll get you a small steak and we won't make you eat it all."

John went to run a few errands and left Mom and me alone. I lifted her right hand and gently held it in both of my hands. "So I've heard that you've been misbehaving."

"What? I don't know what you're talking about."

"Mom, you don't want Isabella to leave you for a minute, not even to take a shower," I said. "What's going on? This doesn't sound like my sweet mama."

"I let her take a shower," Mom said. "Your sister's exaggerating. She's never here anymore."

"Mom, she's always here," I said. "I call her several times a day, and she's always here with you. She's living with you, Mom, all week. Joyce and the kids come over, too, and they are sleeping on the floor, wherever they can find a spot. How can you say that she's never here, Mom?"

"Well, I guess if you say she's here, that she must be," Mom said, defeated.

"Mom, she's here because she wants to be, just like me," I said. "Something's bothering you. What's wrong, Mom?"

"I'm making everyone's lives so hard," she said. "Isabella's living here during the week, you driving every weekend..." Tears welled up in her eyes.

"Oh, Mom, we love you and we are all happy to take care of you," I said. "We're your daughters, and you taught us how to do this. We saw you take care of our grandpa, your sisters and Daddy. You are not a burden. I'm so grateful that you are still here." Tears rolled down my face now. "But I need you to let Isabella take showers, run errands while Angelica is here, OK? Can you do that for me?"

"Yes," she said.

I felt her frustration, and she turned her head away from me. "I'm sleepy. Can you put my mask on?"

***

I heard her bell ringing from the garage, where I was folding laundry. I ran to her side, and she was struggling not to cough. I quickly pushed the bed panel, raised the back of the bed and removed the mask. She coughed for several minutes, and I stood behind her rubbing her back while she coughed. She filled paper towel after paper towel with phlegm and blood. I bore witness to this, trying to stay calm and fight my tears.

"Oh, Mia, it's so scary," she said. "This reminds me of when I had TB." I was holding her hand and longing for something to say to ease her fears, but nothing came to me. I stood next to her helplessly witnessing her daily battle to breath and her slow defeat and it broke my heart to not be able to take this suffering from her.

"Mom, are you sure you don't want me to cook something special for us tomorrow for Easter

Sunday? I can roast us a turkey and make stuffing."

"No, thank you, Mia. I just don't feel like it," she said.

"Okay, Mom, whatever you want. It's all good."

While I was washing Mom's face to get her ready for bed, she said, "I think I want turkey after all tomorrow. There's one in the freezer that you can defrost."

"Okay, Mom, I'm thrilled that you changed your mind," I said. "Can I stop getting you ready for bed so I can check the fridge, and make a quick list of what we'll need from the store? I want to send John out to buy everything tonight, and I'll start cooking before I go to bed."

"Sure, Mia," she said. "Albertson's is open late. There should be bacon in the freezer and maybe some *linguica* for Grandma's stuffing."

"I'll call Isabella and let her know that I'm cooking for Easter and ask her to invite everyone to join us for dinner around 4 p.m. John and I will eat with you guys and then drive home," I said.

"Oh, maybe you shouldn't, Mia," she said. "That's going to be a lot of work for you."

"It will be fine, Mom, and I love cooking for

you," I said and gently kissed her forehead.

I quickly went to the kitchen and took inventory of what we had and what we needed to make Mom her turkey dinner favorites. I texted John the list, and off to the store he went. I called Isabella to give her the Easter Sunday update.

"So Mom asked me to cook her the turkey tomorrow," I said.

"What?" Isabella said. "This is what I'm talking about. I asked her if she wanted to defrost the turkey, and if we had known about it, we could have slowly prepared everything. She's being so selfish."

"This may be the last time she has turkey," I said.

I finished getting Mom ready for bed. She brushed her teeth. I massaged her legs, arms and hands, and changed her nightgown. She took her anti-anxiety, pain and sleeping pills with a little pudding. I got her bed ready, and we started the process of arranging her nine pillows into their proper places so Mom could sleep comfortably. The pillow process was becoming more and more difficult as time progressed. It was now taking almost 30 minutes to get Mom into a comfortable position. She couldn't lie on her side or stomach, and some of the pillows were used to keep her from getting bed sores.

About 10:30 p.m., John returned from the store with everything on my list. I spent the next four hours preparing our Easter Sunday feast. John sat at the kitchen table with his iPad and kept me company. The menu included my Portuguese Grandma Amelia's stuffing, mashed potatoes, gravy, peas, corn, rolls, spinach salad and pumpkin squares. My grandma's stuffing was outstanding, and complex – it included *linguica*, bacon, sweet red peppers, onions, celery, three types of bread, bay leaves and other herbs, and lots of butter. Because Mom was sleeping, John volunteered to taste test the stuffing and had to try several spoonfuls to ensure that I'd gotten it just right.

"I can sample the pumpkin squares," he said when they came out of the oven.

I waved him off before he could cut into the pan.

I knew that if he just had one … he might eat the entire pan. I knew all about John's dessert taste tests, and this was dangerous territory.

Chapter Six

Goodbye, Brown Stove

The day may come when you must

move your loved one out of her home.

It won't be an easy conversation.

Tell her the truth.

And try to not feel guilty.

I'm sure you've made a sound decision

and explored all your viable options.

You are a good caregiver.

Day 147, Monday, May 9, 2011

"They may move Mom from hospice," Isabella said during our morning conversation as I drove to work. Here we go again, I thought, frustrated with the need for yet another evaluation. They were coming Wednesday.

"How is that even possible?" I said. "She continues to decline, lose weight, struggle to breathe, bedridden. ... I can't believe we all have to go through this again."

"They're set up to take care of patients for up to six months," Isabella said. "Nurse Mary agrees that Mom is terminal and clearly needs their services, so hopefully they will let her stay, but they have to evaluate her."

"Have you told Mom?" I said.

"Yes. I told her last night. She was surprised and upset. Poor Mom, she's fighting so hard to stay alive and now this again," Isabella said.

We said our goodbyes, and I parked my car and walked into my office building. My hectic day full of meetings felt like a walk in the park compared to what Mom and Isabella were dealing with today. I said a quick prayer to the Virgen de Guadalupe, asking for her help, and started my work day.

I had a tough time concentrating. I couldn't stop thinking about Mom, her long fight to stay alive. Just when I thought it couldn't get any worse, she'd lose another pound and continue to live, it would get worse. It was so hard to stay positive and grateful for our extra time together when it meant that I watched her deteriorate. And it was exhausting emotionally and physically for all of us. I was finding it harder and harder to juggle my career, care for my sons and arrange my visits with Mom. Around 1 p.m., I conceded, and I asked my boss if I could go home early. The moment I got into the car, the tears gushed. I let them roll down my face.

I drove to a nearby church and went inside. Fewer than five people were scattered through the pews. The dimly lit sanctuary smelled of incense. I quietly lit a candle in front of the Virgen de Guadalupe statue, knelt and prayed for a few minutes. Then I took my seat near the back of the church and quietly wept. The beautiful, peaceful little church worked its magic, and I began to calm down. I imagined my mother sitting with me and holding my hand. I heard her say, "It will be okay. It always is." I knew I had to believe her!

The next few days offered little to keep me calm. A flood of phone calls came from various family members who had heard Mom might be evicted from hospice. I listened to all their concerns and disbelief. My stress soared. I snapped at John, Gabriel and Jessie. I wasn't doing well and it was impacting my entire family. I knew what I was doing, but I didn't know how to stop.

***

"How's Marisol doing?" I decided to focus Mom on the bright spot, her baby great-granddaughter.

"Oh, Mia, she's getting bigger every day." Mom sounded cheerful. "I just gave her to Renee. She drank her bottle with me and fell asleep in my lap. I love having her here with me." As if reading my thoughts, Mom added, "I don't want you girls to worry about hospice. We will figure this out."

But I felt angry. "I can't believe that they might

remove you, Mom."

"You can't be upset, Mia. I was when I first heard about it. But then I thought about how good they've been to me, and I've been in hospice for so long. You know that it's only supposed to be for six months or less."

My dear mom, always understanding of both sides. Even now she had the ability to understand the big picture and be compassionate about people's job requirements and in-place systems, and not take it personally or respond to anyone involved with anger. How did she do this? I still had so much to learn from her.

"Yes I know, Mom, but..."

"Stop, Mia. Don't be angry, and just have faith that no matter what happens it will be OK," she said, and then fell into a major coughing spell. We had to hang up quickly. Her words lingered, and I knew she was right: Faith would get us through this.

Wednesday morning, I dropped Gabriel and Jessie at school and vowed that once I was at work I would not call Isabella every 10 minutes about the pending hospice appointment. Twenty years ago, I had moved away from Santa Maria, to go to college and explore the world. Mom cheered me on and had always been so supportive of my career in high tech. But this is when my heart felt the heaviest about my choice to leave Santa Maria. These moments when I wanted to be there to support my mother but could not because my family and livelihood were somewhere else.

Mom had been sick many times before. So many times I'd had to wait for medical updates and decide if I needed to drop everything and race to be by her side so I could see her one last time. But this was different somehow. Death was no longer the worst news we could get. Death was here, and we were dancing our final dance. We were trying to balance her quality of life vs. suffering, and none of it was easy. "Be present, be grateful" is what I kept telling myself all morning.

Isabella was calling. I jumped from my chair and quickly left my meeting to take the call.

"It's all good, Diana. They are not removing her from hospice."

Tears welled up as Isabella continued. "He was

a super nice doctor. I think he was the director of Santa Barbara County hospice. He explained that because of the time Mom's been in hospice, he had to evaluate her. I guess it's no secret that our mother is a favorite with the nurses and the other support staff, so he had to make sure. And while she is holding on, she is far too ill to not be in hospice."

Day 165, Friday, May 27, 2011

Friday night, I called as I drove home from work, greeted with the news that Isabella had heated up the *caldito de pollo* (chicken soup) for Mom.

"So is Jessie excited about tomorrow?" Mom said when she came on the line.

My son was a huge Giants fan, and the thought that he could go down to the field at AT&T Park and steal second base was thrilling for him. "He is so excited, Mom. I don't think he'll sleep tonight," I said. "I'll take lots of pictures and call you when we get home. I'm sure Jessie will want to talk to you too."

"Will I be able to see him on TV?" she said.

"I don't think so, Mom. They'll take him out on the field in between at-bats during the fourth or fifth inning, during commercials," I said, then added, "I'm sorry that I won't be coming this weekend."

"Oh, Mia, stop. You come every weekend. This is Jessie's 12th birthday gift. Go and enjoy your day with him, and I promise we will all be fine."

The next morning, Jessie got up early. He was dressed, ready to go and buzzing around the house a few hours before we needed to leave for the Giants' stadium. For his 12th birthday, I had offered Jessie a trip anywhere in the United States to celebrate, but he had chosen AT&T Park, the Giants' home, 30 minutes up the road. "I wanted to steal second base," he had told me.

I had jumped on it, doing tons of research. I'd made the reservations back in December before Mom got sick. Then I had given him the news on his 12th birthday, Feb. 11. I delighted at watching him open his final gift that day, seeing his face as it registered that he would get to steal second base May 28 during a game between the Giants and the Oakland A's. He had jumped off the couch.

I splurged and got us club level seats near first base. It was a gorgeous sunny day, and after checking out our seats we headed off to explore the stadium. The game would not start until 1 p.m. I had invited my best friend and Jessie's dad. It was a rare event to have all of us together including John, but today it was all about Jessie.

"Are you ready to go steal second base?" asked the beautiful young woman dressed in a Giants uniform. Jessie's face beamed and he stood up. "You can come with us too," she said as she looked down at me.

"Great, I'd love to," and I strapped my camera over my shoulder.

The young woman led us through a maze of tunnels below the stadium seats as we followed her to the Giants' dugout. Jessie was mesmerized, and we stopped to take a few pictures along the way. She opened a door, and we followed her right into the dugout. It was the bottom of the fourth inning, and the team was there. She found us a couple of seats and explained to Jessie what would happen at the end of the fourth inning. I began taking pictures of the players all around us and struggled to keep my mouth closed and be somewhat composed. Jessie was calm, collected and joyful.

We watched the inning, and Buster Posey was the last player to stand on second base. He was one of Jessie's favorite players. Jessie turned to me with big eyes when he realized that with two outs, Buster was likely to be the final player to stand on the base.

The inning ended and the groundskeepers rushed out to rake the infield and perform other maintenance. The young woman asked Jessie to stand up and get ready. A cameraman stood nearby and began recording Jessie. "The San Francisco Giants welcome Jessie Martin today as he celebrates his 12th birthday and will be stealing second base," said the game's announcer. Jessie's image flashed on the Jumbotron display. Jessie dashed onto the field, dodging players to take the base. Back at the dugout, he brandished the base, and a few players playfully tried to take it from him. All of this was on camera.

"Did you see that, Mom, they tried to take my

base?" Jessie held the base, covered in dusty red dirt footsteps, close to his chest.

The players returned to the field and the young woman led us back through the doors. Jessie was recounting his experience when a middle-aged man in a gray Italian suit approached us. "I need your base for a moment," he said in a very official voice. Jessie looked at me in disbelief. "I'm going to put the official MLB seal on it and officially register it, that's all, and I'll give it right back," he said, smiling and clearly recognizing Jessie's resistance to part with his base. The registration took a few minutes, and once again Jessie was in possession of his base.

When we returned to our seats, Jessie was beaming with pride as he recounted the experience to everyone. The Giants won the game, and it was a perfect day.

Jessie called his grandmother after we got home. "I was in the dugout with the Giants during their at-bat, and Buster Posey was the last player to stand on my base," Jessie told her.

Day 180, Saturday, June 11, 2011

When I came next to see Mom, she was sitting in her chair with the sliding glass door open. "How was the drive?"

"All good and easy, Mom. John did all the driving and Sophia slept most of the way."

"Did Gabriel and Jessie stay with their dad?" Mom asked while Sophia chased Lulu in their happy reunion dance.

"Yes, they're spending the weekend with him. He's cooking at a school carnival and the boys are going with him."

The dogs began to bark loudly.

"I'm sorry I can't hear you," Mom said as she scrunched up her face and adjusted her hearing aids. "They are so happy to see each other."

I joined Sophia and Lulu on the floor and began to toss a squeaky hotdog toy, and they both raced to retrieve it and return it to me. Little Gigi climbed into my lap and let the two alpha dogs run around and chase the toy. It was no use trying to talk to Mom until the roughhousing was done. She giggled as she watched the silly dogs play.

Sophia and Lulu finally wore themselves out and stretched their furriness near the sliding glass door to cool down. "Has Gabriel started football practice?" Mom said now that the dogs were quietly panting and resting.

"Yes, I think he likes the socialization more than the playing. It's been super hot, and it's a rigorous program. So we will see."

"He'll be OK. It's good for him, Mia."

Mom had encouraged me to let Gabriel try out for the freshman high school team. I wasn't a big football fan and worried about concussions. When my little brother had played in high school, a serious injury had changed the direction of his life.

"Want to see pictures? I have Gabriel's eighth-grade graduation and Jessie stealing second base." I hoped to change the football subject.

I knelt next to Mom and placed my laptop on the arm of her chair. "Oh, Mia, Gabriel is so handsome in his royal blue cap and gown. He looks so grown up. I can't believe that he'll be in high school in a few months. How I wish I could have been there." Mom looked longingly at the pictures.

"He and his best friend cleaned up the garage so we could have their party. We managed to barbecue in the rain, but our house isn't big enough for 36 kids to hang out, so they decorated the garage," I said. "They were all so well-behaved, and they had so much fun."

"How did you do all this, Mia? Coming to see me and having a party at your house for 50 people? I'm so worried about you." She reached out for my hand.

"I'm okay, Mom. John is a huge help at home, and Gabriel and Jessie have been so good. I just feel terrible that I haven't been able to come and see you for a few weeks." Now I tried not to cry.

"Mia you've done so much for me. Your boys need you, too. Please don't feel bad," she said.

I struggled to hold my tears. Mom was so sweet, compassionate and loving. How was I going to live in a world without her love in it? "Here, look at Jessie, holding second base."

"He looks so happy," Mom said. "And Buster Posey, that's my favorite player, too."

Dusk fell, but it was still warm. "Mom, it's too

hot to cook tonight. John is going to pick up dinner for us. I've been craving Chinese food," I said as I closed my laptop. "I'll cook for you tomorrow morning."

"Sounds good, Mia. But don't get too much. I can't eat the way I used to," she said as she touched her tummy.

"Just eat as much as you can, Mom. I know you have to save room for your Krispy Kremes." There, I had made her giggle, but I could see that she was tired.

I went through the process of putting the mask on her. Mom's face had oozing sores from the ridges of the mask, and I tried to be as gentle as possible as I placed it over her nose and mouth. I saw her grimace with pain. She quickly looked up at me to reassure me that she was ok. I reminded myself that this wretched mask was keeping her alive. I blessed her forehead and watched her quickly fall asleep.

***

Mom ate about eight spoonfuls of Chinese food, a whole lemon-filled Krispy Kreme doughnut and milk.

"Mom, do you want to learn a new game on the iPad?" I said. "I know that you are playing solitaire on it, but there are some other games that you might enjoy too."

Mom had loved to play solitaire and had gotten too weak to play with cards, so Isabella had taught her how to use the iPad, and she loved it.

"Do you think I can learn how to play it?" she said.

"Of course, it's super easy," I said as I reached for the iPad and powered it up. I leaned over the side of her bed and began to teach her to play Harbor Master.

"Oh, Mia, there are boats everywhere, I can't get to all of them," she said, giggling as she swiped her fingers as fast as she could. At last, she said, "What happened?"

"The boats crashed into each other, and it ended the game. Do you want to play again?"

"Yes, this is fun, Mia."

Early Sunday morning I started cooking: fresh orange rice, Peruvian beans, guacamole and chicken fajitas. I had marinated the thinly sliced chicken breast strips the night before in a garlic, vinegar and California chile paste. I added sliced onions and red peppers and cooked them on high heat.

"The house smells yummy," Mom said after I removed her mask.

"I made you chicken fajitas, fresh beans, rice and guacamole," I said. "I got up early so the house would still have a chance to cool before it got too hot again."

"Oh, Mia, thank you. How will I ever repay you for all of this?" she said, reaching for my hand.

"You already have, my awesome sweet Mom."

I was cleaning up the kitchen when Isabella arrived to relieve me and take over for the week. At first I was busy explaining what food I'd cooked for Mom, where the leftovers were and how to serve fajitas. Isabella was quiet, and I noticed that she had been crying. "Are you okay, Sis?"

She signaled me to follow her into the garage. "Mom hears everything," she explained. "I don't know how she can't hear you when you're right in front of her and won't wear her hearing aids, but she hears everything when you're in the kitchen or one of the bedrooms and you don't want her to hear. She has bionic distance hearing or something." Isabella ushered me into the garage and closed the door.

"Joyce and I got in a big fight. It's just so hard for us," she said of her life partner. "We don't spend any time together anymore. And Joyce and the kids come over during the week, but our children are sleeping on couches, on the floor. It's a mess. We have a huge house and yet we're trying to hold our family together and live here and there, and it's just not working."

Tears streamed down Isabella's face.

"Oh, Sis, I'm so sorry. None of us expected Mom to live so long. I'm sorry I can't be here more to help out during the week and I haven't been able to come down the last couple of weeks," I said. "Do we need to move her to a nursing home? To your house?" I hugged her.

"You know how she feels about leaving her house," Isabella said. "We've asked her to move in with us so many times before. No, on the nursing home, but I think it's time to move her to our house."

I took a deep breath and looked around the garage for a moment.

"I think that's best, Sis, it's time," I said finally. "Will you speak to her? I know Mom doesn't want this to be hard for you."

What I was about to say next was very hard. I wanted to be tender, but honest. "Mom is being selfish right now, but you know in your heart that this isn't our sweet Mama. She's in total survival mode. I know you understand this more than me. She's reverting to being a child, to being completely self-absorbed with surviving another day, and we are losing her. And it's not that she doesn't care about how hard this is on all of us. It's that it's not her priority anymore. I think if we tell her what's really going on she will be okay with us moving her out of her house." There, I had said it. Those words had been a long time coming.

"I don't think she'll go," Isabella said sadly, "and she's going to be super upset about us wanting her to move out. I'm afraid to talk to her."

"Bring it up, and if she's completely against the

idea then I will talk to her." I hugged Isabella again.

When we returned from the garage, Mom was holding Marisol on her lap. "She's going to be three months old this week," Mom said, smiling. "She's a good eater and sleeper and such a happy baby." It warmed my heart to see them together, and I was so grateful that Mom still had the strength to hold her. "She's rolling over. And look at her smile!" Mom continued, but John was at my ear, saying, "Babe, we need to get going. The traffic is going to be terrible, and Gabriel and Jessie will be home by 7:30 p.m."

I turned to him and nodded yes.

Our goodbye ritual began. I kissed Mom and blessed her. Marisol, too. I hugged Isabella goodbye, and yes, the tears started up again. I didn't even realize that Lulu and Gigi had followed me out, jumped into the car and were waiting for me.

"They've been doing this lately," I said to John, shaking my head and rolling my eyes.

"We should just take them. They'd be so happy with us and little Sophia. They would go on walks every day, get tummy rubs and gourmet doggie food from you," John said.

For now, those dogs needed to stay with Mom. I scooped them off the seat.

"Did you forget something?" Isabella shouted from the kitchen when she heard Mom's front door open.

"Nope, just returning Lulu and Gigi," I said. "They tried to stow away again."

"Those little escape artists," Isabella said.

On the way up the coast, John asked about what would happen to the dogs after Mom passed on.

"Isabella will be keeping them," I said.

"Really? Diana, those dogs would be so much happier with us," John said. "We love dogs."

"You know I've tried."

"I don't like it one bit, Babe." He surprised me with his insistence. "They should come with us. Those dogs don't leave your sight. They sleep with you, and I know that you're the only one that ever walks them."

"We will see," I said. "Right now, I'm just trying to keep the peace."

"Honey, those dogs won't survive with your sister," he said. "This is something you should fight for!"

But I had horrible memories of my father and his siblings fighting over my grandparents' belongings when my grandma died. I was seven years old when we went to pick up my grandpa to move him in with us. "When we arrived, he was sitting on his front porch with his clothes and personal belongings around him in paper bags," I told John. "An aunt and uncle were clearing out his house and didn't even put his stuff in a suitcase. My dad pleaded with them to give him a bed for my grandpa, and they wouldn't. He'd lived there for more than 30 years. He was grieving my grandma that he'd been married to for more than 60 years, and his children wouldn't give him a suitcase or a bed. It was awful, and I can't be one of those children who disrespects my mom's wishes. As much as I love her dogs, I can't do this because it's not what she wants."

The traffic was terrible, and we were late getting home. I was exhausted. My shoulders and neck ached all the time now from the stress and driving. Gabriel and Jessie were clearly annoyed with us for being late, and they needed to take showers and go to bed for school bright and early Monday morning. As I lay in bed later that night I couldn't stop thinking about how hard this was on all of us. And no matter how much we sacrificed and tried to help my sweet mama, we weren't going to like the outcome. I guess some journeys must be taken even if they bear no fruit. But I needed to figure out how to make this all a little more bearable for all of us.

***

Monday morning, I checked in. "Did you talk to her about moving?" I asked Isabella during my drive to work.

"Not yet. I know she's going to refuse and be upset," Isabella said.

I swallowed hard. "Sis, you have to. You need to tell her how hard this is for you and your family. She will understand. Don't feel guilty."

Isabella promised to do it later in the week, but deep inside I knew she would not be able to persuade Mom to leave her home.

Day 201, Saturday, July 2, 2011

This week, my father would have been 96 years old. As I drove with Sophia to Santa Maria, I wondered about my dream about her party. Was my father really getting ready for her?

Along the highway, I spotted a young doe with her fawns. It made me recall memories of my dad and his deer hunting mishaps. My dad killed more deer with his car than he ever did hunting them. Poor Daddy was so blind, I don't think he ever shot a single deer. He'd go on deer hunting trips occasionally, and someone would always give him a deer or part of a deer because they felt sorry for him. But with his car, now, that was a whole other story.

Once when I was eight years old, we were at a family barbecue at Lake Cachuma. Daddy had to work in the morning, but he was going to drive out and meet us in the afternoon. It was about 45 minutes to drive. The party was so much fun. My cousins grilled tri-tip on oak wood, and my mama made her famous chili beans. The table was filled with salads, desserts, guacamole, salsas, grilled buttered French bread and the rice that we called Spanish rice then,

before my sons had come al

rice. Someone had hired a

remember what we were c

food was amazing and ou

events, and there was lo'

children to play with.

About 3 p.m., Mom came to me wearing a nervous look. "We're going to go look for your dad," she said. "He should have been here hours ago, and I think his car might have broken down. Your *niño* is going to drive us."

Mom, my godmother, my little brother and me got into my godfather's car and started driving down the windy road that hugged the edge of the lake. We had driven only a few miles when we saw a highway patrol car and a tow truck. Mom's panic-stricken face and teary eyes told me Daddy might be seriously hurt. My heart began to race so hard that I thought it was going to jump out of me. We pulled over to the side of the road and got out of the car. There were a few people gathered and we saw Daddy and a giant dead buck in the middle of the road. He rushed to greet us.

"Damn buck, didn't even see him," he said. "He

cross the road as I came around the

tried to miss him, but as you can see I hit

"Where's our car?" Mom said.

He walked over to the edge of the cliff and pointed down at Cachuma Dam. Fifty feet below was Daddy's white four-door Impala, crushed on a giant rock.

"I was able to get out of the car and climb back up to the road and flag for help." He looked sheepishly at my mother. "Darn lucky that I didn't land in the water."

Mom blessed herself, and there wasn't any more conversation about the deer incident.

The tow truck pulled the Impala up the embankment. While the car was full of dents, it still ran. One of our cousins lifted the dead buck onto the back of the truck, and we all went home. Mom and Dad skinned the buck on our basketball court, and in came the carcass to our yellow Formica kitchen table, where Mom cut it into steaks, roasts, etc. I helped her wrap and label the cuts of venison and place them in the freezer. Her father had been a butcher, and Mom knew her way around a carcass.

That yellow Formica table had seen many a carving — beef, sheep, pigs and more. And I was always there helping her. My parents were strong then. Able to butcher animals, work hard on the farm, care for us, go to parties and dance. I clearly didn't understand the blessings of healthy parents back in those days.

Midway to Santa Maria Sophia and I stopped in King's City for a Starbucks, and soon, Lulu and Gigi greeted me at the front door with friendly licks and wagging tails.

"Are the Giants winning?" I said as I entered and I sat down next to Mom for a few moments.

"Yes, they just scored two runs," she said.

I checked to see if she had water.

"Did you bring me any doughnuts, Mia?" She was like a child asking for candy.

"You know I can't come visit you unless I bring some Krispy Kreme. Do you want a lemon one?"

"Yes, please, with a little milk. And can you please hide a few for me. Joyce's kids eat my lemon doughnuts, and you know how I love them. I'm not being stingy, but the lemon ones are my favorite and they can eat the other ones. Don't you always bring two dozen?" Her eyes grew wide, again the small child asking for dessert before dinner.

"I brought fresh red snapper," I announced. "I'm going to make you fish tacos with black beans."

I had prepared the beans at home the night before, adding onions, red peppers, fresh garlic, bay leaves and *linguica*, a yummy Portuguese sausage.

"Did you bring some avocado for the tacos?" Now I heard the master chef voice.

"Of course I did," I said. "I'm your daughter."

In the kitchen, I started dinner. I prepared the spicy breading for the fish. I combined cornmeal, spicy California chile powder, granulated garlic, dried onion flakes, salt and pepper, and set it aside. I made Mom's orange rice and chopped all the veggies for the tacos including jalapeño and serrano chiles, tomatoes, cilantro, lettuce and avocados. Then I went to the garage to fold laundry.

From the garage, I heard the frantic ringing of

Mom's bell. Running to her, I saw her frightened face. She signaled for me to remove her mask.

"I'm going to raise your bed, and I'll get it right off you," I said.

She nodded her head yes. I gently removed the mask from her face, put the oxygen cannula back into her nose and placed the hose behind her ears. She started coughing. It was clear that she had been trying to hold it in. I rubbed her back as she coughed repeatedly for five minutes. At the end of it, she had filled paper towels with blood. I held her hand as she gasped for breath.

"Mia, I will be okay," she said. "It's just so scary when I have the mask on and I need to cough."

Then her sad eyes registered on my face. "Oh, Mia, look at you, you look so tired. I didn't even notice before. You have black circles under your eyes.

This must be so hard for you," she said. "It's too much, you coming every weekend."

Now was the time. "I actually wanted to talk to you about that, Mom."

I took her hand. "Mom, I think it might be time for you to move in with Isabella. You always promised that you would when it was time, and I think that time has come."

"I don't want to leave my house, Mia," she said calmly. "It's just so hard to live in someone else's house. Your sister already talked to me, and I told her that I'm not ready and I don't want to go." She was pleading now.

"I can't even begin to understand how hard this must all be for you, Mom, but I need you to think about Isabella and what her life will be like when you're gone. Her staying here all week is hard for her and it's creating issues with her and Joyce. It's not good for them to be apart so much," I continued gently.

"Well, she comes over and the kids sleep here sometimes, too," she said.

"Mom, the reality is that their relationship might not survive this," I said. "Do you want Isabella to be alone after you die? I know that's not what you want. She's been doing this for seven months. It's a long time, Mom. I'm sorry to be so frank, but I'm concerned, Mom, and I felt like you needed to know the truth."

My heart sank with sorrow as I watched tears stream down her face. I waited for her to speak.

"I don't want that for Isabella," she said. "This is so hard on you girls." Now she was sobbing. "I'm such a burden on you."

I took a deep breath. "Mom, that's not what I'm saying," I said. "We both adore you and will do anything we can for you, but we need your help, too, and it will be a huge help to both of us if you are living at Isabella's." There, it was said.

Mom was quietly crying. She turned her face away from me to the window, but she still held my hand.

"Okay, Mia. I guess it's time for me to move."

Chapter Seven

Lulu Runs Away

You may become unreasonably angry.

The grief, sadness and stress may impede

your ability to be rational.

If this happens to you, just let it out.

Don't try to hold it in.

I found going to a vacant field,

kicking the dirt and crying out loud

until I couldn't cry anymore to be very helpful.

Find a way to let the anger run out of you.

Day 214, Thursday, July 14, 2011

The headaches had been crushing me, only I wouldn't say it. They were persistent, a constant low-grade pain for two weeks. Finally, it was John who had had enough.

"It's time for you to go to the doctor, Babe," John said.

So I'd promised him, and now here I was, trapped in an MRI tube. My heart was racing and it felt like it was about to jump out of my chest. And I started to hyperventilate.

"Oh, please get me out of here!" I screamed.

The technician tried to calm me down. "Can hold on for a few minutes? It will be OK," he said. But it was no use, and he had to get me out. The life-size tube was too much for me. I was seriously claustrophobic; a condition I'd had all my life.

They gave me anti-anxiety pills and a new appointment for the next day.

John didn't think twice about taking the time

out to drive me to the appointment. But he added, "I think you should consider staying home this weekend and resting, Babe. We could take the boys go-karting and relax. Gabriel is starting high school in a few weeks, and it might be good to have a weekend without Santa Maria before high school starts."

But Isabella was in the middle of moving Mom to her house. I knew she needed me.

"She has lots of other people helping her, Diana," John said. Before I could argue, he said, "And none of them are working full-time, live four hours away and are raising two teenage sons."

That seemed to settle it. I could tell that John was worried about me, so I finally conceded. I would take a weekend off from visiting Santa Maria.

The hard part was telling Mom the truth about my headaches.

"Oh, Mia, why hadn't you told me? Two weeks, and you have it all the time?" she said when I called.

"Yes, Mom. I remember when it started, it felt like an explosion in my forehead. That day I was putting towels away. I lay down for awhile. It got less severe, but it didn't go away. I've tried various medications, but nothing has worked."

"Why didn't you tell me?" she asked.

"I didn't want to worry you, Mom," I said. "You have enough to deal with, and I'm sure I will be OK."

"Diana, I'm still your mother and I need to know if you're sick." She sounded hurt.

"I'm sorry, Mom," I said. I waited a few moments and let the silence linger. I knew it would only make her more annoyed to hear any more of my reasoning. Then I needed to tell her. "Mom, I'm going to stay home this weekend. I have a lot to take care of with Gabriel starting high school in a few weeks. I'm sorry…"

"Stop. You need to take care of yourself, Mia. You are doing so much for me," she said. "I have so many leftovers in the freezer. Rest and do something fun with Gabriel and Jessie." I knew she was right. I needed to rest and spend time with my beautiful sons and John. She was wise and loving. Oh, sweet Mama, why were you dying?

***

John and I took Gabriel and Jessie go-karting

on Saturday and had a late lunch. They had a great time picking out their official racing helmets and learning how to drive the fast go-karts. Once on the track my sons were transported to teenage boy heaven, 60 minutes of speed. The go-karts could go up to 40 miles an hour, and Gabriel, Jessie and John went flying by me lap after lap with roaring engines and burning rubber. When the race ended and it was clear that I came in last place, they all had a great time making fun of how slow I drove—poking fun and asking me if I knew the objective was to get around the track as fast as possible. I'm not a speed demon, and I was completely out of my element trying to drive a go-kart. But for that hour I forgot about Mom's impending death and enjoyed playing with John, Gabriel and Jessie. We all needed this fun afternoon.

Day 237, Saturday, Aug. 6, 2011

By the time I returned to Santa Maria, Mom's move to Isabella's was in full force. Boxes were packed in the garage. I leaned in to kiss Mom's forehead as Sophia, Lulu and Gigi chased each other in circles through the house. Sophia had snored the whole way — me, too, according to John. Now she was bouncing off the furniture, delighted to see her running mates. I paused to watch them play, but then my eyes landed on the blank walls. Many of Mom's knickknacks were packed away. We were a week out from the move.

I could feel Mom's sadness, as I chatted to catch her up about current events, my job and my sons.

She broke in. "Mia, what do you want? It's best to take whatever you want now."

"Mom, you gave me Grandma's magical molcajete years ago. I use it all the time and I don't want anything else." I felt my shoulders fall back and lowered my gaze to the floor.

"Do you want any of my furniture?" she said.

"No, thank you, Mom. Our house isn't very big, and we don't need anything," I said.

She looked offended, and I felt terrible.

I thought about it some more, and offered, "You know, Mom, when you're ready to part with them, I would love the little boxes I've bought for you from my travels, some of your angel statues and the Nativity I bought you. And of course, any family pictures you want to give me. But Jessie's already scanned them all, so we have digital copies, too."

Mom continued trying to justify the gifting of her household furniture. "I'm giving Renee my kitchen furniture, and Isabella's going to put my big TV in her house, and of course she's taking my bed and dressers. She bought me my mattresses a few years ago."

"Mom, really, it's okay." I took her hand. "I'm not upset about your things. Please give them to whoever you think needs them. My grandma's molcajete was all I wanted, it's okay."

Mom reached to the side of her nightstand and handed me a manila envelope. "Here, this is for you."

Inside was the Mother's Day card I had made her in kindergarten. It was made of faded red construction paper with two stick figures with triangle bodies and stringy hair holding hands, a large heart and the words LUV MOM written poorly. Then I saw the Christmas card from first grade, a paperweight with my second-grade picture, grade school report cards and class pictures. I placed the envelope over my heart.

"Isabella and I have been going through all my things, and I thought it was time for you to have these," she said.

"I loved making my little art projects for you, Mom," I said as I held up my lopsided snowman with a rectangular torso. "I never was a very good artist, though."

Then my eyes fell on a black-and-white photo of me, about two years old, plopped on the floor playing with an Australian shepherd dog. "I don't remember ever seeing this picture," I said. "What was this dog's name?"

"Butch, I think." She smiled at the memory. "We had lots of dogs named Butch."

I remembered we had lots of Australian shepherds, too. "I used to love watching the Australian shepherd dogs round up the cows from the fields," I said, picturing these enormous Holstein milking cows on our farm. "The dogs would bring them into the milking barn for Daddy. The cows were about 50 times bigger than the dogs, and these dogs would bark and bark and bark until they chased them into submission.

And they were lightning fast even when the fields were muddy. It's as if they had invisible wings on their paws."

"Your dad had some great cow dogs," Mom said, smiling.

Then she turned a bit sad. "I remember that day you found Rusty, your golden retriever," she said.

"I was five years old, and we were outside playing fetch," I said, a feeling of sorrow growing inside of me. "He disappeared suddenly, and when I called him, he didn't come. I started looking for him and when I saw him laid out next to the oak tree in the backyard, and he wasn't moving, I started screaming for you."

"He must have been bitten by a baby rattlesnake to have died so quickly," Mom said. "He was still warm when I checked him."

We saw lots of snakes growing up on the ranch. I nodded at Mom as we shared the memory. "I'll never forget that time we came home from Mass, and there was a rattlesnake coiled up on the step just below our front door. We were screaming, and you calmly went around the side of the house. It seemed like forever for you to come back around. When you did, you had a shovel. You whacked that thing. You beat and beat, and then you chopped that snake into small chunks. All while still in your church clothes." I couldn't help giggling at the picture in my mind.

"My dad used to kill them, skin them, barbecue them," Mom said. "I knew the head had to come off first, and that's what I did." Mom smiled like a schoolgirl.

"And, oh my, do you remember when Francis and I got chased by the bulls, and we had to climb the oak trees?" I said. "I think I was six and Francis was four."

"I told you not to go to that field, over and over again, and that those bulls could kill you." Mom shook her head. "But you wouldn't listen."

"Mom, they were never in the field," I said, picking up the story. "We knew they lived in the hills, but we never saw them in that huge, inviting field behind the house. I remember hearing them at night sometimes, but I had never actually seen them until that day. There were six of them, and they must have all weighed over 2,000 pounds. Francis and I were playing hide-and-go-seek, and all of a sudden we heard them charging us. The ground was literally shaking."

I could remember it like it was minutes ago. "The barbed-wire gate was too far away, so we each climbed a tree, and we hung on for dear life. We had to cling to those trees for hours and hours while the bulls stomped, bellowed, kicked dirt and basically terrorized us. We were both crying our eyes out and screaming for help, but no one came. The bulls must have finally gotten tired of torturing us and left. But Francis and I stayed in the trees for what seemed like at least 30 minutes to make sure they weren't tricking us. Then we slid down and ran the entire way home."

"You were too far away for us to have heard you, Mia, and you were a mess when you came home, covered in dirt, tears and snot all over your faces. Your dad wanted to punish you, but I just couldn't," Mom continued the memory. "And you were only gone for about an hour, Mia. Oh, how you exaggerate sometimes."

"Mom, for a scared six-year-old girl, it seemed like a lifetime," I said. "I think I still have bull post-traumatic stress disorder. But it was also the first time I remember you making us crunchy tacos for dinner. The tacos made me forget the day's bull drama and calmed me down."

"I think that's why your dad made you show that champion at the fair all those years later, to get back at you," Mom said, smiling.

I had been 14, and the champion bull weighed 2,300 pounds. He wore a ring through his nose. "I had to carry an electric cattle prod to move him along," I said. "That walk around the arena was the longest walk of my life."

My father had said, "Don't be afraid. The bull will smell your fear, and it will be really bad for you."

Mom laughed and laughed at our stories, until she started coughing and our fun was over. Mom slouched forward in her chair and tried to catch her breath in between wet roaring coughs. She was filling her paper towels with phlegm and blood.

"Can I bring you anything?" I said as I rubbed

her back gently. I felt helpless once again knowing that Mom was losing her battle to breathe.

When she stopped, I said, "Do you want to take a nap?"

"Yes, Mia, I think that will help me. We had such a nice talk today." She held my hand and I bent down to kiss her forehead.

Then I wired all her oxygen tubing and gently placed the mask on her face. She grimaced as the plastic edges touched her skin. I absolutely despised putting it on her. It was impossible to put her mask on without placing it on new or healing sores.

In the kitchen, I started dinner: crunchy beef tacos, Peruvian beans and orange rice. I cooked the ground beef in a large skillet, fried rice in a second pan and fried bacon in a third. I made guacamole and toppings for the tacos — chopped cilantro, onions, tomatoes, lettuce, jalapeño and serrano chiles. The kitchen heated up from all the cooking, and I felt happy. It was fitting that I was making her famous tacos this last weekend in her home. And as I fried the tortillas, I thought about the copious amounts of love my sweet mama had poured into her amazing recipes here in this kitchen. I knew that I'd always be connected to her through her food, even when she was gone.

When John entered the kitchen, his eyes grew wide at the array I was preparing. "Babe, you realize that she's only going to be able to eat one taco."

But I knew Isabella's family would eat the leftovers. I also knew Isabella could repurpose the leftover meat and beans to make Mom a taco salad and tostada later in the week. I explained my thinking.

"But I'm running out of ideas of what to make her, John," I added. "You saw her. She continues to lose weight and interest in food." Tears welled up in my eyes.

"Oh, Babe, I didn't mean to upset you," he said as he came over to the stove and hugged me.

Ring, ring, ring.

Mom.

I raced from the kitchen.

At her side, I removed her mask and rewired her oxygen cannula.

"Oh, Mia, it smells so good in here," she said. "I smell beans, rice and maybe ground beef with onions.

Are you making me crunchy tacos?"

"Yes, I am. Dinner won't be ready for a while. Do you want a little snack? And no, I'm not giving you a doughnut right now."

"Yes, Mia, I'm a little hungry," she said.

I returned with a small plate of Peruvian refried beans, topped with a little grated cheese, salsa and guacamole.

"Oh, Mia, this is so good," she said as finished her bite of the homemade bean dip.

"I'm glad you like it, Mom," I said.

A couple of hours later, as John predicted, Mom ate just one taco and apologized for not being able to eat more. I cleaned up the kitchen, and later we watched Meryl Streep in *It's Complicated*. Mom laughed out loud several times.

"It was such a good movie, Mia. I loved it. She's such a good actress," Mom said.

"Yes, she is, and I'm thrilled that you enjoyed the movie," I said.

Early Sunday morning, I started a simple chicken soup based on the recipe of my dad's mother,

Grandma Amelia. She had taught Mom how to make it before she passed away, and it was one of my dad's favorites. Mom had combined it with her spicy Mexican chicken soup recipe and created a delightful soup with veggies, potatoes and rice. She made it for us whenever we were sick, and it always made us feel better. The spices sent our colds running. But today, I thought it should be milder for her.

I didn't add any chiles and went light on the garlic, too. She wasn't eating enough, and although she didn't say anything about the spices, I wondered. I knew she could add salsa if she wanted more heat. I sautéed onions, fresh tomatoes, celery and garlic, then added the cubes of raw chicken, plus a bit of water, a small can of tomato sauce, raw long-grain rice, chopped carrots, diced zucchini, fresh lime juice and Knorr chicken broth. I let it all simmer. And chopped cilantro and fresh avocado that were a great garnish for the soup. By the time Mom woke up it was almost finished.

"You don't sleep, Mia." She shook her head at me. "It's not even 7 a.m. and I smell soup. Look at your eyes and those dark circles." I didn't have the heart to tell her that my low-grade headache still hadn't gone away and it was making it hard for me to sleep.

"I'm fine, Mom," I said. "I wanted to make your soup early when it was still cool outside so that I didn't make it all hot in here for you."

"It smells like your Grandma Amelia's chicken soup," she said.

"Yup. I decided to make her version instead of the Mexican one with chiles and squash," I said. "A nice change, and it's not spicy. There's salsa in the fridge and chopped avocado if you still you want to sass it up a little. Do you want to taste it?"

"I'll have some for lunch a little later," she said. "Would you bring me my banana and coffee so I can take my pills? Oh, and can you bring the remote?"

Mom watched Mass on TV while I finished the soup and cleaned up the kitchen. She seemed distant this morning, and I wondered if it was because I was leaving later or because she was moving soon. She'd been living in her three-bedroom, two-bath ranch-style home for 15 years—she had moved there shortly after my father died. The quiet cul de sac was surrounded by similar homes with longtime residents who all knew and adored Mom. The more I thought about it, the more I knew that her distant demeanor was because of her upcoming move.

At the grassy field near the neighborhood school, I let Gigi, Lulu and Sophia out to race on this gorgeous summer day. Lulu and Sophia vied for first place. Gigi was happy to stay close to me and let the other two compete for top dog. Watching their tiny legs run and their ears flop up warmed my heart. They were all panting and exhausted when we arrived home, heading straight for the water bowls. They flopped down on the floor next to Mom's bed. Isabella was here.

"You're going to give these poor dogs a heart attack," she said jokingly.

"They're fine, Sis," I said. "They had a blast on their walk. Now they'll sleep all day."

While Mom was preoccupied with the San Francisco Giants game, Isabella signaled me to follow her to the garage, where I saw stacks of boxes.

"She doesn't want me to get rid of this stuff,"

Isabella said. "She's still hoping she'll be coming back here someday."

"I think you should get rid of as much as you can," I said firmly. "She's not coming back."

I asked my sister where she would store it all.

"In our backyard," she said. "I just can't take her hope away."

Tears welled up in Isabella's eyes.

"She knows, Isabella," I said, trying to mask my frustration and concern regarding Isabella's inability to accept Mom's terminal diagnosis. Pretending that her move was temporary and that she may return to her home didn't help anyone, least of all Mom. "She understands. But it's your call. I'm sorry I can't help you with the move. I have to go to Gabriel's high school functions next weekend. I can't miss them."

"Don't worry." Isabella hugged me. "We have lots of help lined up."

I looked forward to a weekend at home with John and my sons. Gabriel was delighted I was attending his freshman events. At this point, Mom had been in hospice for nine months. My low-grade headaches hadn't gone away, and after MRIs and several doctor visits, I had no diagnosis other than what I already knew: It was a chronic headache. They had no idea how to treat it. Of course, I was relieved it wasn't a brain tumor, but somewhat annoyed that it was my constant companion. My doctor tried to explain that Mom's prolonged terminal illness and my current work-life schedule was most likely the cause. Doctor's orders were to slow down and relax a little. John and my close friends had the same advice, to pace myself. Mom had already surpassed her original life expectancy by nine months. But how could I slow down while Mom was still alive?

After Mom was settled in her new quarters, I called.

"Everyone has been so nice," Mom said, trying to be cheerful. "My bed's in the den right next to the kitchen, and my chair is here, too."

I heard the sadness in her voice. "I'm sorry I couldn't help. The new-parent reception was really nice last night, and Gabriel had a blast."

"You had to be there, Mia. And your sister had lots of help," she said, and then was silent.

I felt a knot in my stomach about all she had lost. "Well, Mom, I just wanted to check in on you and say goodnight. I'll call you tomorrow," I said and ended our call.

I knew Mom didn't feel like talking about being moved to my sister's, and I felt too much guilt to make small talk. My mom's losses were piling up: All her siblings were gone, my dad — and now her home. I didn't know how to make her feel better.

Most days, I could muster the energy to be joyful and cheerful. Most days, I focused on celebrating the fact that I had a mother for one more day. But tonight I just couldn't.

Later that evening, Isabella filled in the picture, much of which I already knew. Mom was seriously depressed about the move, and Isabella felt terrible for forcing her to leave her home.

"Isabella, stop," I said. "You couldn't continue. Your family was falling apart. Mom is lucky you were able to take care of her for so long, and that you're a nurse. If it weren't for you, Mom would have spent the past nine months in a nursing home. I would have never been able to take care of her like you have, or survive not working and so on. Don't beat yourself up, Sis. She'll be OK. She's a survivor. That's why she's still here. I know she loves you and appreciates all you've done for her."

"Then why do I feel so awful?" she asked, and I could hear the tears in her voice.

"Because, no matter what we do for Mom, how much we care for her, cook for her, et cetera, we're still going to lose her," I said, and paused a moment so Isabella could process what I had already accepted. "And even though she's still with us, we lose her a little every day as she becomes more and more dependent on us. Her survival instincts dominate her choices. There's no easy way to witness this, Sis. We just have to be grateful that she's still here and know that we're doing our best."

The next few days Mom was massively depressed and withdrawn, making it almost impossible to converse with her on the phone. Isabella was equally distressed with Mom's behavior and felt massive guilt. And I was in the Bay Area working, caring for Gabriel and Jessie and trying to sort out how to improve this situation from afar. I just had to find a way to help everyone feel better.

The following weekend, Gabriel and Jessie accompanied me to visit Mom. Isabella's house was full of loud children, little Marisol, small adorable dogs chasing each other and me cooking. Surrounding Mom with life and noise lifted her spirits. Isabella's house was cheerfully decorated in bright colors and had brilliant sunshine. Mom's hospital bed was in the kitchen/great room. Her bed was next to the large kitchen counter that was surrounded by stools. She was now able to actually be in a kitchen again. And there was a large great room with her huge flat-screen TV, which made it easy for her to watch the sports teams and novellas she enjoyed so much. We hosted a family barbecue Saturday, and the house filled up even more.

My master taste tester advised me on preparing the chili beans for the barbecue. As I fed her a spoonful, I said, "At least now, I don't have to worry about you going behind me and seasoning my beans without my knowledge."

"What are you talking about, Mia?" Mom said.

"Time to fess up, Mom," I said. "I know that you secretly always reworked my beans and added more spices.—I'd leave the room for a minute and I'd come back and my beans would be a different color, and they would taste different. Now you can't do that, and you're just going to have to teach me your magic! Although if you could figure out how to move your hospital bed over to the stove, you would."

"Oh, they're so good, Mia. You need to add some more cumin and chile powder. I like the *linguica*. My chili beans don't take *linguica*, but it's a good add," she said.

Linguica is spicy Portuguese pork sausage. I'd grown up eating it with eggs or as an appetizer at barbecues. I'd started adding it to beans recently, as it added a nice subtle flavor like spicy ham. I was thrilled that Mom agreed.

"I can never remember if it's cloves or cumin," I said. "And Mom, you know that I always have to add my Portuguese sass to most of your recipes." I knew Mom would agree that it was hard for me to always honor all the ingredients of her sacred recipes. Most of my attempts to alter her recipes didn't work, and I'd return to her original masterpiece, but oh, to finally have a winner.

Mom tasted the beans a few more times until she gave me her final nod: These beans approved by a master chef.

I returned to chopping onion for the orange rice.

"Oh, Mia, what I would give to stand next to you in the kitchen one last time," she said.

My heart sank. I hadn't been prepared for that one. I laid down my knife.

"I feel the exact same way, Mom," I said, trying to hold back the tears. "I've loved every minute of our cooking."

The whole family, all 20 of us, sat down with Mom in the great room for a yummy barbecue dinner. There weren't enough chairs, so some of the family stood and others sat on the floor. No one cared about the informal, somewhat uncomfortable arrangements—it was good to all be near Mom. Our older brother grilled all the meats on my sister's oak-burning grill on her patio. Our menu included grilled tri-tip — Santa Maria's world-famous beef cut similar to a roast — chicken, grilled French bread with lots of butter, chili beans, orange rice, potato salad, salsa and guacamole. It was a feast, and the house smelled amazing with a combination of oak smoke and all the other dishes. It reminded me of the many barbecues we'd had growing up on the dairy farm.

"Look, Grandma, Marisol loves your beans," Renee said as she fed baby Marisol a few bites of mashed-up chili beans in her high chair. Marisol was trying to take the spoon from her mother.

"Beans are so good for her, Mia," Mom said. "And I think your *Aunt Diana's* beans are actually better than mine."

"Oh, stop, Mom, no way," I said. "Yours are absolutely the best ever."

After the kitchen was cleaned up and most of our extended family left, we sat in the den with Mom and watched *How to Train Your Dragon*. Mom loved it.

Everyone went to bed, and I slept next to her on an overstuffed couch.

"Your visit really helped Mom get out of her

funk," Isabella said as she helped me load up my car Sunday afternoon.

"I think it helped Mom to realize that your house is more accommodating for us to all hang out together, and she's basically in the kitchen, so I think she's starting to ease into her new digs," I said.

As I kissed Mom goodbye back in the house, I gave her my instructions: No cooking. No new recipes until I returned the following weekend.

"Oh, Mia, if only I could," she said, smiling. And how I wished for that too, for Mom and I to stand side by side and cook together one last time.

As I watched Gabriel and Jessie kiss their grandmother goodbye, I could read their thoughts: Each time they parted ways, they wondered if it would be the last time. They both looked terribly sad as we walked out to the car.

But we were all surprised to see our stowaways waiting for us. Lulu and Gigi were in the car with Sophia, settling in for a ride.

"Did you forget something?" Isabella asked as she heard us come in the front door.

"Nope, just returning Gigi and Lulu," I said.

"They are always trying to go home with us. And one of these days, I'm just going to take them."

Day 254, Tuesday, Aug. 23, 2011

"Did you know Barry Bonds went to my new school?"

Gabriel was speaking to his grandmother on the phone. I'd picked him up from football practice, and he'd called her on our drive home to tell her about his first day of high school. But he hung up quickly and put his phone away.

"She's coughing too much, so we had to say goodbye," he explained.

"That happens to me, too," I said. "I'm not sure why, but she gets more coughing attacks while she's talking on the phone than when she's in person with you."

Gabriel looked out the window and was quiet the rest of the drive home. I wasn't sure if he was crying.

At dinner, Gabriel shared more about his first

day as we ate grilled hamburgers. Jessie asked his older brother tons of questions, and while they were talking, it hit me that Jessie would go there, too, but he would never get to share his first-day experience with his grandmother, not like Gabriel did today.

"What's wrong?" Gabriel broke into my thoughts. "You look sad."

"I'm just tired," I said. "It's been a long day."

Day 296, Monday, Oct. 3, 2011

"Lulu is gone."

Isabella was crying into the phone.

"What? She died?" I said.

"No, she ran away," Isabella said. "There was a small hole in the backyard fence and she got out. She did this once before, but a neighbor brought her back a few days later. But this time we can't find her."

"How's Mom?" I said.

"Not well. She's really upset."

Isabella told me that Joyce and her teenage

son Lucas had been walking the neighborhood trying to find Lulu, with no luck.

My mind raced. "I can't get to Santa Maria for another four days, Isabella. I just can't skip work tomorrow. I'll post a picture of Lulu to Facebook. You need to do the same, and the kids too. Do it right now! I'll call you back in a few minutes."

I hung up the phone quickly. I began going through all my pictures on my phone to find a picture of Lulu. Thankfully I had lots of great photos of her. I quickly posted a picture on Facebook with a plea to look for her. I tagged friends and family who lived in Santa Maria.

"Babe, Lulu's missing? Really?" John said as he came racing into the bedroom after reading my Facebook update.

"I know, Babe, you told me to take the dogs," I said, anticipating what he would say next. "She slipped through a hole in the backyard gate." I couldn't help it. A tear rolled down my face.

"I'm not upset with you, Babe, I'm just pissed," John said. "I knew something like this would happen."

"Mom, Lulu is gone?" Gabriel said as he came

into my room.

"Yes. Can you please post something to both your Facebook walls with the picture I posted?" I said. "Right away."

"Mom, this is going to kill Grandma," Gabriel said. "You know it is. We need to go down there right now and help them look for her."

"I can't, Gabriel," I said, feeling the twinge. "I have big meetings all week, and work has been so flexible with everything with Grandma. I just can't, and you have a football game on Saturday. Update Facebook — and pray, Gabriel. I'm going first thing on Saturday morning, and hopefully they'll have found her by then."

Gabriel walked out of my room looking disgusted. John sat next to me on our bed and updated social media. I was grateful for his company. Little Sophia jumped on the bed and snuggled next to my legs, like she knew she was needed. She must have sensed my anxiety.

I was direct when I called Isabella a bit later. "Okay, John, Gabriel and I have all updated Facebook. Why haven't you guys done it, Isabella?"

"Well ..."

"Isabella, you know that minutes matter. Just use my photo. And make the kids do it now."

I was pissed.

She agreed.

But an hour later, I didn't see it on her Facebook wall. I had to vent to John. "She still hasn't updated Facebook." I felt helpless.

"Why are you surprised, Babe? She doesn't want the whole world to know that your mom's dying and somehow one of her precious dogs got out on her watch," he said.

"Wow, I hadn't even thought about that angle," I said. "I went straight to how could we get the word out ASAP." I knew I had to smooth things out with Isabella later and apologize for my abruptness.

Just then I noticed that Isabella had updated her Facebook wall. I breathed a sigh of relief.

Now I needed to know how Mom was doing with all of this. I called to check on her.

"Oh, Mia. I knew about that hole in the fence, and I told Joyce that Lulu might get out," Mom said. "She already had once, and she said she'd covered it."

I could hear that Mom was trying to hold back tears.

"I made everyone put it on Facebook, Mom, and hopefully someone has seen her or heard something," I said. "Joyce is making flyers, too, with her picture and putting them all around the neighborhood. They are going to call all the dog pounds tomorrow morning as soon as they open." I hoped that sounded like a good plan.

"Do you think we'll find her, Mia?" Mom said.

I hesitated. "I sure hope so."

On Saturday, Sophia and I headed to Santa Maria, knowing that nothing had turned up a lead on Lulu. My heart was heavy. Lulu, and her constant companion Gigi, meant so much to Mom. She would meticulously prepare their area on her bed every night before she went to sleep. She'd lay out a special blanket and cover them up like babies. When Mom could no longer drive, Lulu and Gigi were the only living creatures she'd interact with for days and sometimes weeks. They were her family. Lulu was the oldest, and Mom favored her over Gigi, although she'd deny it.

I arrived earlier than usual, but when I saw Mom's face, I felt like my heart would break. Mom had clearly lost more weight in the past week.

"I'm going to look for Lulu," I said about why I had gotten there early. "I'm taking Gigi and Sophia to see if we ~~see~~ spot anything or hear her bark..." I started to share my plans, but Mom was crying.

"You're not going to be able to find her," Mom said. "She wasn't wearing her collar."

Now tears streamed down her face.

"What? Why wasn't she wearing her collar? Are you sure?" I said.

Mom cautioned me to lower my voice. "Shh, they're upstairs," she said with a finger over her lips. "Joyce had been complaining that Lulu and Gigi's collars made too much noise and took them off days before Lulu ran away. So you see, Mia, there is no way for anyone that may find her to return her to me." Now she was crying openly.

"What?" I shouted, but then held Mom as she wept with grief. I decided to say nothing more about the collar.

I leashed Gigi and Sophia and headed out, Sophia leading, Gigi following closely. We walked every street of Isabella's neighborhood. Several dogs barked at us from their yards, but we never heard little Lulu's familiar bark. Both dogs were breathing heavy and needed water when I returned to Isabella's house.

"Sorry, Mom, but we didn't hear her or get any clues," I had to report. "I'm going to take Sophia and go to your old neighborhood. I've heard so many stories about dogs making heroic journeys back to their homes. Maybe she's made it back to your street, Mom. It's only a few miles."

I kissed her on the forehead and left.

Once in my car, I called John to vent about the collar. I told him I was driving to Mom's old street, and he thought it was a good idea, but he added gently, "I think you need to start to accept that you're not going to find Lulu."

Walking door-to-door on Mom's old street, we turned up nothing. The neighbors all inquired about Mom's health and were saddened to learn about

Lulu's disappearance. Holding out hope, I gave several of her old neighbors my cellphone number and they promised to call if they saw Mom's beloved companion.

I felt a wave of grief to see Mom's vacant house. The landlord had been working on it, and I peered through the windows and saw that she'd painted the inside and replaced the floors and carpets with hardwood floors. I walked into the backyard to look around, but I saw no signs of Lulu. Then it struck me: This would most likely be the last time I'd ever be in Mom's backyard. In that instant, I could no longer hold back the realization of Mom's impending death. My tears were volcanic.

I ran to the car with Sophia and started driving, crying loudly. I drove for many minutes, and before I knew it I parked in front of the long road to the dairy farm where I'd grown up. I had no idea how I'd gotten there. I hadn't been out to the ranch for years. Our house had been torn down, and there were just a couple of barns left. Fields of strawberries stretched out where once cow pastures and fields of alfalfa and broccoli had been.

I got out of the car and walked to the gate. It was mid-afternoon, and the wind was blowing as it always did at this time of the day because it was close to the ocean. I started kicking the dirt and screaming. "WHY? Why this? Why now? Hasn't she gone through enough? Her Lulu! What kind of God are you?" I screamed into the blue sky as if I expected an answer. I eventually fell to my knees in despair, and there I began to accept that Lulu was gone.

"I couldn't find her, Mom," I said, back at Mom's side, holding her hands in mine. "I'm so, so, so sorry."

"Thank you for trying, Mia," Mom said. "Lulu's so cute, I'm sure some family snatched her up and they're not going to return her."

I sat next to her and held her hand quietly for a few minutes.

Then I told her that my older siblings, Augustine and Lena, and her best friend Maria were coming for dinner. "I'm going to make us barbecue shrimp."

"Oh, Mia, are you sure you want to do that for

so many people tonight? You look so tired," she said, then gave me that knowing look. "I know what you're trying to do."

"Guilty as charged. I'm trying to cheer you up with food," I said. "I learned from the master."

Chapter Eight

A Birthday For Rose

Be present.

Don't focus on this being her last birthday.

You'll have time to miss her later.

While your loved one is still breathing

and in your presence, be there,

cherish her

and do your best to make her

smile and laugh.

Day 311, Monday, Oct. 17, 2011

Mom loved the iPad game Harbor Master, which I downloaded for her. But as I was driving home on Highway 101 one evening after work, she told me she stopped playing it. "It was making my heart race."

I felt guilty. "I'm sorry, Mom, I didn't mean to teach you to play a game that would be bad for your heart."

"It's okay, Mia, it was fun. Trying to keep all those boats from crashing into each other is really hard. Mine crashed all the time and it was just too much for me." Her voice was full of warmth. "How would you know that it would stress my heart?"

"Pretty darn cool that you tried it, Mom," I said, grateful that my mother could still make me smile. "My mama and her iPad games. Who knew you'd become a gamer in your old age?"

"Oh, Mia, I need to stick with Solitaire," she said. "It doesn't affect my heart, and it's much more my speed." Then I heard a nervous pause. "Do you think I'm getting addicted to gaming?"

Once we established I was just kidding her,

she relaxed, marveling at technology and slipping into a memory about our first black-and-white TV.

"Do you remember how Daddy used to use me as his remote control?" I said. "He'd have me turn the TV dial for him, stop and continue. Thankfully we only had three channels on the ranch or he might have kept me there forever."

I loved hearing her giggle on the other end of the line.

"Gabriel and Jessie don't even know how to turn on a TV without a remote control," I continued.

"Really, you don't think they do?" she said.

"They couldn't find the remote last year during the World Series and were freaking out because they couldn't turn on the TV," I said. "I was running late from work, and when I got home the entire living room was a disaster. The cushions were off the couch, the furniture was pulled away from the walls. It was pretty great to walk in and turn it on the old-fashioned way by hitting the power button on the TV, and then using the cable box to manually find the channel. So yes, I know they can't."

Mom was laughing, too, and unfortunately it

turned into a giant coughing spell. She apologized as she hung up to try to catch her breath.

My heart sank. I knew that we were on seriously borrowed time and soon there would be no more daily calls with Mom. We had logged so many miles together talking about my jobs, Gabriel and Jessie, movies, current events, etc. Tears filled my eyes at the reality of our journey nearing its end. It felt like we were in the last five minutes of the last act of our lives together. I believed with all my heart that Mom was going on to heaven and would be reunited with her family and friends, but how was I going to manage my long commutes without my best friend?

Remembering it was October, I turned my thoughts to what this month meant to me. Every year I dreaded it. My Uncle Frank, Grandma Magdalena, Aunt Aldena and my adorable Grandpa Alfred all died in October. I was always afraid that Mom would die during this month too. With just a few days left in the month, I was on high alert that Mom might join that list. Her birthday was in nine days, and often Mom would talk about how her mom died just three days before her birthday, and my grandpa died three days after her birthday. So far, she hadn't mentioned it this year, and I wondered if she was thinking the same thing. In the past, I would have just asked her.

But not now. Our relationship was slowly changing. More and more, I self-edited almost everything I said to her, trying to find words that wouldn't remind her she was dying.

I did my best to embrace the fact that she was still here. Noticing this change made me feel lonely. I longed for our pre-hospice days.

The moment I pulled into the driveway, I was snapped out of my melancholy. Gabriel ran out to greet me with Sophia, and I was thrown into an evening of cooking dinner, learning about my sons' day, playing with Sophia and visiting with John. Now more than ever I cherished coming home to a full, bustling house.

I would be returning to Santa Maria on Friday, for Mom's birthday. Jessie decided not to go, and John offered to stay home with him.

It would just be Gabriel and me.

Day 315, Friday, Oct. 21, 2011

Gabriel was checking in with Doc Burnstein's Ice Cream Lab to see if Mom's birthday cake was ready. Arroyo Grande was still at least 90 minutes away, and if we hit any traffic, we might not make it.

"They close at 9 p.m., Mom," he said. "They said that they'll be cleaning up until about 9:30 p.m., so just knock on the door if we get there after closing. They'll let us in."

What a relief.

"Can't you just pick it up tomorrow?" Gabriel said.

That was possible, but I had a lot of cooking to do. "I wanted to get this out of the way tonight and not worry about it tomorrow," I said.

"Why aren't you making her one of your ice cream cakes? Yours are awesome, Mom," Gabriel said.

"No time, Gabriel," I said. "The ice cream needs to be on the cake for a minimum of 24 hours, and I couldn't transport it already made all the way to Santa Maria, or make it when I got there, so this was really my only option. Grandma loves Doc Burnstein's ice cream, and I know she'll love that we bought her an ice cream cake."

We pulled in just in time – 8:55 p.m. The clerk was super-nice, and we were out in just a few minutes. I put the cake into the ice chest with the rest of the food for Mom's birthday party. We would celebrate a few days early because I couldn't be there on the 26th.

Isabella greeted us at her front door when we arrived at 9:30 p.m., and went straight upstairs to her bedroom to relax with Joyce. Her embrace lacked enthusiasm and sadness was obvious in her eyes, which were swollen and surrounded by dark, deep circles. She was exhausted and stressed. Caring for Mom all week was clearly getting harder.

"Hello, beautiful birthday girl," I said, giving Mom a kiss on her forehead as I entered the great room on Isabella's first floor.

Mom struggled to hug me from her hospital bed. As Gabriel bent down to hug her, I could see he was shocked at how thin she was. She had lost about another 10 pounds in the past couple of months and she barely resembled herself.

But when Gabriel said, "Hi, Grandma! How are you?" I could see he was trying to be brave.

"I'm doing okay, Gabriel," Mom said. "I think you've gotten even taller since the last time I saw you. How tall are you?"

"Maybe a little," he said. "I was 6-foot-2 when they measured me at my football physical last month."

"Well, I think you're taller than that now," Mom said, holding his hand. She looked at him adoringly, trying to soak up all of him. "Do you have a girlfriend?"

"No, I don't have a girlfriend, just friends," Gabriel said. "We bought you a cake from Doc Burnstein's, Grandma. Rocky road."

"I love rocky road," Mom said.

I could see how uncomfortable Gabriel was making small talk with his grandma, but I was grateful for his effort as he continued to converse with her. When a sudden coughing spell seized her, Gabriel's big eyes expressed fear.

"I need to sit her up," I said, racing to her bed. I reached for the control panel to raise the top of her bed quickly.

"This might last a while, Gabriel," I said after a minute. "Why don't you go upstairs and hang out with Joyce's son Lucas for a little while?"

I held Mom and rubbed her back, and she continued to cough uncontrollably. She filled several paper towels with phlegm and blood. Gabriel quickly left the room, and I suspected he was crying. I didn't know how to help him with his grief, and I couldn't ask my best friend for advice. Tears filled my eyes. It was yet another example of the giant hole Mom's death was leaving in my life.

Stop crying now, I kept telling myself as I held Mom. I tried to wipe the tears off my face. You can't let her see your tears, and she's right here, right now. You will have plenty of time to cry when she's gone, the nasty little voice in my head continued. As crazy as it sounds, that voice helped me get my composure back. I managed to stop crying.

"Thank you, Mia. Can you bring me some water?" Mom said and leaned back in her bed.

I headed to the refrigerator. "Do you need anything else? Your inhaler?"

"No, thank you, I can't use it again for a few more hours," she said. "I think my coughing spell scared Gabriel."

"He'll be okay, Mom," I said. "Your coughing spells scare all of us." I placed the straw in her mouth.

"They scare me too, Mia," she said, looking away.

There was dead silence for a moment. I didn't know what to say. I couldn't tell her that she'd be better soon. That would have been my normal response. I couldn't say she'd be in heaven soon and never have to cough again. Oh, how I need a dialogue writer next to me, telling me the exact right thing to say to this amazing woman who meant so much to me. For some reason I was off balance tonight, struggling to be my joyful, positive self. Was it October? Was it the reality that it was her last birthday? Seeing Gabriel? Isabella?

Mom at last broke the silence. "Gabriel is so grown up and so handsome, Mia."

"Do you remember what you said to me when you first saw him?" I said.

"That he was beautiful?" Mom said.

"No, you said that he weighed more than a 10-pound sack of *papas*! I was like, Mom, seriously, I just gave birth to your grandson and you're comparing him to a bag of potatoes," I said. "Not who he resembles, how gorgeous he is … *papas...*"

"Oh, Mia, I don't remember that at all. I think you dreamed it. He was a beautiful baby, lots of dark curly hair, beautiful skin and a smile that lit up the room."

"He was pretty adorable, and I had so much fun with them when they were young," I said. "He's a good kid, but teenagers are tough."

"It doesn't end there, Mia," she said. "You're always going to worry about them. It's what mothers do."

It was time to get Mom ready for bed. The ritual of helping her brush her teeth, cleaning her up a little, emptying her catheter bag — these were easy tasks now. However, the pillow orchestration was getting harder and harder. It took about a half hour to get ten pillows in their correct places because of her bedsores. I was grateful they weren't infected.

When I'd finally gotten Mom comfortable, I

brought her pain and sleeping pills with a little piece of her favorite — a lemon-filled Krispy Kreme doughnut.

"You thought I forgot to bring them, didn't you?" I said as I handed her the treat.

"No, I saw you sneak them in while Gabriel was talking to me," she said, smiling.

I wired her the mask, blessed her forehead, covered her shoulders with blankets and stared at her for a few minutes as she fell asleep. I was in awe of how she continued to live like this. I knew she was suffering so much, yet she managed to be kind, loving and gentle. How did she do that? I had to find the courage to ask her.

I slept next to Mom's hospital bed on a giant sectional couch. It looked comfy, but the six square sections moved every time I did and some part of me kept trying to fall through the cracks. I didn't sleep well. I missed sleeping at Mom's house in her comfortable bed, but I wasn't going to bring that up. Sophia and Gigi slept with me too. Between their snoring and Mom's oxygen compressor, it sounded like a den of elephants.

My mind raced, and sleep eluded me. When I

was in high school, I remember going into my mother's bedroom at night. I'd lie on her bed or the floor and do my homework. She was a remarkable speller, and she often proofread my homework and corrected my spelling mistakes. My mom had been my first spell-check, and she was so good at it. But this was back in the day when I had to type some of my homework and use white-out and tape to make corrections. Gabriel and Jessie had no idea how much harder homework used to be, before computers, laptops and iPads.

During baseball season, Mom would read the paper in bed and listen to the San Francisco Giants games on the radio. I loved hanging out in her room with her. As a lifelong Giants fan, Mom had often said that she couldn't go to heaven until they won the World Series, and thankfully, they had in 2010. She was a huge 49ers and Lakers fan, too. I shared her love of baseball and the Giants. I wasn't an athlete and was always the last child picked to be on anyone's team in the schoolyard, but I understood the mechanics of the sport, scorekeeping, etc. So much so that I became one of the varsity baseball stat girls in high school, which earned me my letter — and that was all because of Mom and our late nights with KNBR and the Giants.

Later it helped me get selected to lead a very cool video project with Major League Baseball and meet Bud Selig, the commissioner of baseball in New York.

What a fun phone call that was to make to Mom and tell her about being in the headquarters, the replicas of all the stadiums, how beautiful and magical it was in a big high-rise in New York.

The other best phone call was the day I met the Rock, Dwayne Johnson, while touring the WWF facility for another video project. He was so nice, tall and remarkably handsome and personable. He later sent me life-sized signed posters of himself. I had given one to Mom, as she was a wrestling fan. I wonder what happened to the poster. Her love of sports was something that had brought her tremendous joy. Hardworking mother, housewife, master chef and sports junkie — that pretty much summed up Mom.

I was smiling, recalling the joy I'd had sharing

my various work adventures with Mom. She had always been so proud. She understood how far a journey I had made from my humble dairy farm beginnings to the amazing career, travel, people I'd met. No one else ever would understand this about me the way she did.

Then I heard her moving in her sleep — and I was transported back to the room, sleeping next to her hospital bed, the night before her last birthday celebration. I felt unbearable grief. I cried myself to sleep.

Day 316, Saturday, Oct. 22, 2011

Mom was ringing her bell.

I woke up quickly and raced to her bed. "Good morning, beautiful birthday girl. Happy birthday to you, happy birthday to you..." I sang to Mom as I removed the mask and rewired her oxygen.

"Thank you, Mia," she said as she smiled and held my hand.

"How are you today?" I asked.

"I'm good. You don't sleep, Mia." I heard the regret in her voice. "I'm sorry that I woke up so early."

"Mom, don't worry about me," I said. "I'm fine, and it's a big day. I have some major cooking to do for your birthday party."

"What are you making?" she said.

"I'm making guacamole, salsa as appetizers, crunchy pork mole, orange rice and beans," I said proudly.

"I love crunchy pork mole, Mia," she said. "It's my favorite."

"I know, that's why I'm making it for you. It's also your hardest recipe, so I'm going to need you to stay awake this afternoon to walk me through it. So, early nap for you today, otherwise you might end up with mushy pork mole." I enjoyed teasing her.

"It's not that hard to make, Mia," Mom said. "I know you can do it without my help. But if you want me to supervise, I will."

"Yes, I need you," I said emphatically. "And I'm making you a proper birthday breakfast, and don't make one of your faces, not hungry, etc. I'll be making it much later when everyone wakes up, and it's not a lemon doughnut. You can have that as a snack later."

"I guess I'll let you be the boss today."

I brought Mom her morning juice, coffee and banana, and I watched her count out her morning pills. I didn't really understand how she continued to remember her daily meds schedule. No one did. Diminished lung capacity was supposed to make people brain foggy, but not Mom.

The hospice nurses guessed that Mom had been living with only three lung lobes — instead of the normal five — for almost 60 years, and her body, more important, her brain, had adapted to function well when science said otherwise. It would be just like my mom to be the exception.

I was so grateful that although her body was failing, I could still talk to her and she could still engage with me. Although I was sharing less and less because I didn't want her to worry, we had this. She was still here with me. I understood right then that saying goodbye to her this slowly was a true gift and today, her last birthday, I was going to make her the best food ever, because that's how we truly shared our love with one another.

Gabriel entered the kitchen and greeted me with a sleepy voice — then he saw Mom was awake, reading her paper. "Good morning, Grandma, happy birthday!" He went to her side and they began to chat about his school and sports. Gabriel seemed calmer this morning and more himself with his grandma than the night before. I was proud of him for being able to converse with her the way he always had. But as I watched them, I focused on how frail her frame was. Our attempts to keep her from losing more weight were failing. That thought felt frightening.

I started to fry bacon as they chatted away. Isabella, Joyce and all the children were home, including little Marisol, who was now seven months old and eating real food, so I decide to make two whole pounds. Bacon was a family favorite, and if there was any leftover, I could use it in our beans later on.

"Hey Mom, bacon smells good." Gabriel was back in the kitchen.

"Bacon and Grandma's yummy French toast," I said.

"Do you need any help?" he said.

"No, thank you. I've got this. I'm sure Grandma would love to continue your conversation."

I turned to the French toast batter: Bisquick, eggs, milk, cinnamon and vanilla mixed into a large bowl. It was basically pancake batter that I made a little thinner. I put two slices of cinnamon bread into the bowl and let it sit for a few minutes so it could absorb the batter. I pulled them out and placed them into a large frying pan with butter. The French toast cooked quickly, and they looked deliciously golden brown when I removed them from the skillet.

I made Mom a plate with a single slice and a couple of pieces of bacon, and gave Gabriel the other one. By the time I started cooking the other two slices, the family had all woken up and milled into the kitchen for their breakfast. Bacon and French toast aromas with a hint of cinnamon – an amazing alarm clock.

"It's so good, Mia, but I'm sorry. I just can't eat anymore," Mom said.

"It's okay, Mom. I know you're saving room for that doughnut later," I said as I collected her half-eaten plate.

Gabriel looked my way as he saw how little his grandma had eaten. He rushed into the kitchen behind me and whispered, "Mom, you need to make her eat more. Look how skinny she is."

"I can't, Gabriel," I said. "She eats what she can. I know she's trying, and I make her food that I think she will force herself to eat. She doesn't have much of an appetite."

"I think you need to force her, Mom." He wasn't going to relent.

"If only I could."

From the other room, I heard Mom say, "Marisol is sure enjoying your French toast."

We turned to watch the baby in her high chair, joyfully feeding herself one piece at a time with her chubby little fingers.

"Yes, she is."

Isabella's daughters, Joyce's two teenage children, Mom's 25-year-old grandson and nine-year-old great-grandson, Adam, gave Mom a hug and wished her a happy birthday. I was proud of our family as I watched everyone interact with Mom. None of them mentioned anything about it being her last birthday or looked as if they were holding back tears. It was the unsaid truth, and every one of them chose to be joyful about spending one last birthday with her. I knew they were all grieving in their own darkness with their friends, but today they were grandchildren celebrating their grandma's birthday breakfast. And it was a lovely thing to be a part of and to watch.

The kids helped me clean up the kitchen. Isabella and I helped Mom out of her hospital bed and into her chair. She was so weak, and moving her out of the bed was getting more and more difficult. But we managed and she was happy sitting in her chair, surrounded by her family.

"Are you starting to make dinner already?" Gabriel asked as he watched me put the giant pork loin on the counter.

"Yes, it's going to take me pretty much the rest of the day to make Grandma's crunchy pork mole, rice, beans and guacamole."

I washed the pork loin and placed it on a giant cutting board and started the task of cutting into small one-inch-by-one-inch cubes. The family retreated to the upstairs a few minutes later, and Mom and I were left alone in my sister's great room.

"Mia, that is such pretty meat, there's so little fat," Mom said.

I held it up for her to see. "It's a pork loin from Costco. It has this giant piece of fat running on the side and I bought some fresh *manteca* to use to fry the pork in, just in case this isn't enough." The *manteca*, or pork lard, seemed just the right touch.

"I usually use the pork shoulder when I make crunchy pork," Mom said.

"I know, but I thought this would be easier to cut up, and hopefully it will still be yummy," I said. "The shoulder has lots more fat, and I've seen you sit at my table for hours, meticulously cutting up pork. I just don't have that much time today."

"Oh, Mia, once again you just came to work," Mom said. "I worry about you."

"I'm fine, Mom, and happy to cook for you, especially on your birthday," I said. "I just hope your crunchy pork turns out okay."

"You're such a good cook, it's going to be delicious," she said. "Everything you make is so good." I felt tears well up in my eyes. She was my master chef and I'd spent decades as her student, and now it was graduation and I would never be returning to her classroom. I treasured her compliment and tried to hide my tears. There was just one recipe that I'd never learned how to make. It was too late, and she would die without me ever learning to make my favorites, her flour tortillas.

"I wish I'd mastered your tortillas, Mom. They are the best, and they are so good with mole."

Mom had made flour tortillas her whole life. It was her big chore after she came home from school to make the tortillas for the working men who stayed in the boarding house her mother operated. Mom could go through 50 pounds of flour in just two days.

We had made them together thousands of times. It was the first recipe that I'd ever made with her, when I was only nine years old. I'd tried so many times without her — and failed every time.

"I think I can only make tortillas that are edible when you help me," I told her. "Making the dough without measuring anything like you do, and just going on how it feels, is beyond me."

"You'll figure it out someday, Mia," she said.

"Your sister knows how to make them."

"I know, and she doesn't even like to cook. Anyway, maybe you're right and I'll figure it out someday," I said. "Tonight, I'm sorry to say, your amazing crunchy mole will be served with store-bought tortillas."

"They're good too, Mia."

"My favorites were those super thick ones you'd make for after-school snacks sometimes. They were about half an inch thick, slightly crunchy on the outside, light and fluffy on the inside, and you'd poke holes with a knife and fill them with butter. OMG, those were amazing. No wonder I was a chubby child and loved food so much. It's all your fault."

She was watching me cut the pork, and I remembered how my parents had given me a rolling pin in a giant box of spices when I married. "That was the best gift ever. I think I still have some of the bay leaves and cloves. They lasted longer than my marriage."

Just then, the doorbell rang.

"Hello, Rose! Happy birthday!" It was Carolyn, one of Mom's hospice nurses. "I had to come by and see you. I hope I'm not interrupting."

They exchanged hugs, and I quickly learned that Carolyn had used her day off to see Mom. "She's one special lady," Carolyn said, holding my mother's hand.

As they chatted, I continued to cut up pork. My mother's love was like a magnet. Watching them, it hit me like a tidal wave. Today was her last birthday. My eyes welled up and I moved to the farthest corner of the room. "I need to take this call," I said, holding up my phone. I ran out to the front yard and sat on the small bench on the porch. I hadn't even washed my hands. They were smeared with pork grease. I was pretty sure that was unsanitary. I made myself get up and go to the side of the house, where I washed my hands under the hose. Then I returned to the bench, lost in grief, tears streaming down my face.

"Hi, Diana."

It was Judith, another one of Mom's hospice angels.

"Are you okay?" She hugged me.

"Just having one of those moments," I said, openly crying. "Today is her very LAST birthday. And I know I need to be grateful that she is still here with us...but I just know how much I'm going to miss her."

Judith listened and gently stroked my arm. "Your mother is a very special lady. It's my day off, and I'm breaking the rules by being here today, but I had to come. Diana, she is still here. And you must know how lucky you've been to be her daughter."

"Carolyn's in there with her now and said the same thing about having to come visit her today," I said. "I know I have to make this a great day for her. I'll get it together, but I just needed a moment. Poor thing, she's so thin now and she can't cook with me anymore. And she barely eats anything I make for her. I know she tries. But she's so much worse. And every time I leave on Sunday, it's the same. Will I ever see her again with her eyes open?" I was crying like a small child.

"Your mother adores you, and she's so proud of you and is always talking about you and your sons," Judith said. "She wishes that you didn't have to see her go through this. As hard as it is, stay present with her. And don't focus on making this the best birthday ever or it being the last birthday, but focus on the gift it is to be with her." Judith handed me a tissue.

"You guys are such angels," I said as I took the tissue. "Here I was having a serious pity party about my dying mother, and you walk up and say exactly what I needed to hear."

I cleaned up my face and walked back in the house with Judith. "Look who I found outside, Mom."

"Happy birthday, Rose," Judith said as she gave Mom a hug.

The three women were quickly lost in conversation, and I returned to my 10 pounds of pork loin.

"Mia, is there any more French toast?" Mom said.

"Yes there is, Mom. I have some bacon, too," I said.

"Heat it up for them, Mia. They're both too skinny and they need to try your yummy French toast." She continued in food-pusher mom style.

I made each of them a plate with a slice of French toast and a little bacon, and they sat on the couch next to Mom's chair and ate their late breakfast.

"I knew you guys were hungry," Mom said as she watched her dear nurses gobble up their food.

"It's so yummy," said Carolyn.

"It's my mom's recipe," I said.

"Yours is better than mine ever was," Mom said.

"It's the cinnamon bread that makes it so yummy, but it's your original recipe, Mom." I continued to cut up the pork.

"That's a lot of pork," Carolyn said. "Are you making *chile verde*?"

"No, I'm making my mom's favorite, crunchy pork mole. It's amazing. I'm making tons, as you can see. I'll make sure that we save you some so you can have some during your next visit with Mom."

"Your mom shares your cooking with us all the time," Carolyn said. "Everything you make for her is so good. We had some of your crunchy tacos a few weeks ago. I even took one home to my husband."

"Mom taught me."

After they left, Mom needed to nap but asked me to wake up her when I started the mole. "I want to watch you."

"Of course, Mom. I'll make the beans, rice, and the guacamole while you get your beauty sleep."

I gently placed the mask on her face and rewired her oxygen, but she had several open oozing sores, and there was absolutely no way to avoid them no matter how gently I placed the mask on her face. She grimaced.

"I'm okay," she said, sounding like she was in a tube.

As she slept, I tried to focus on the joy of cooking for her, but the oxygen compressor and the mask were so loud, it was challenging. I put on headphones while I prepared the beans and rice to get into the cooking zone: first salsa, then Marc Anthony.

I put the dried *pasilla, nuevo mexico, ancho* and *guajillo* chiles in a soup pot with onions and garlic to rehydrate them. I had boiled the Peruvian beans, and they were ready to be refried. I chopped a pound of bacon into small pieces and fried it until it was golden brown. Little Gigi and Sophia were hovering nearby, hoping for a little piece of bacon. I took a few pieces out for them to cool before adding two serrano peppers to the frying bacon and fat to give the beans a little spice.

Next I started Mom's delicious orange rice. I fried the washed long-grain rice in oil, and when it was golden brown turned off the burner and left it on the stove. This was Mom's tested shortcut that I'd never tried. She'd heat it briefly before adding the chopped onion and all the liquid ingredients, hours later. It was always amazing, so hopefully it would work for me, too.

I placed the beans into the frying bacon, and it sizzled when the beans hit the bacon fat. I started smashing the beans with a potato masher once they were bubbling and added a little salt, pepper and a little granulated onion to the bubbling Peruvian bean goodness. They smelled amazing. The kitchen was humming, the familiar smells of refried beans and rice were working their magic, and my mood lightened. They had brought me back to finding the joy in this day. We were having a party with yummy food, and we were celebrating our beloved mother.

Next was the guacamole. I chopped onion,

cilantro, tomatoes, serrano and jalapeño chiles. I removed most of the seeds from the chiles because I didn't want it to be too spicy. I placed everything into a bowl and squeezed in fresh lime juice. The avocados were perfectly ripe. They were a lovely shade of green as I cut them in half, with no overripe black or dark spots present. I scooped them out of their skin and placed them into a separate bowl. Then I added fresh lime juice and salt, then mashed them up. I added the ingredients from the other bowl and tasted it. Just like Mom's — delicious!

"It smells like Mom's kitchen," Isabella said as she entered the room.

"The beans and guacamole are done, and the rice is started," I said. "Do you want to taste the beans?"

"Sure, just a spoonful. I'm still a little full from breakfast," Isabella said, lowering her voice when she noticed Mom was still sleeping. "Why haven't you started cooking the pork? Doesn't it take hours?"

"She asked me to wait until she woke up. She wants to watch. So, dinner might be a little late," I

said.

"Oh, it's okay," she said as I handed her a spoonful of beans. "You have to wait for her."

"These are so good," Isabella said. "But this isn't Mom's recipe."

"Tia Juve's refried Peruvian beans," I said. "I prefer them over pintos, and Mom's had them before and loved them, too." Peruvian beans are a cross between pintos and white beans. "When I make them, I add a little onion like Mom used to do to her white beans, so I guess it's some of Mom's recipe now, too. There's guacamole and salsa in the fridge, too."

"You are so fast. I can't believe you made all this in the past few hours," Isabella said.

"Well, I brought the salsa from home, and I boiled the beans this morning. It's really not that much," I said. "What time is everyone coming over?"

"Around 5:30," she said.

"Yikes. Even if she wakes up now, the mole won't be done until around 7 p.m. or later."

"Don't worry," Isabella said, "they can get started on guacamole, chips and salsa. Trust me, no one will care if dinner is a little late."

"Can you stay down here another 30 minutes, so I can take a quick shower, Sis?"

"I'll turn on the baby monitor and watch her from upstairs. I can get down here and take her mask off as soon as she wakes up. That's how I do it at night," she said.

"That's right, I forgot."

Mom woke up to the smell of beans, rice and chiles. But when I came over to kiss her, what she noticed was my scent.

"What perfume are you wearing? You smell good, too."

"Daisy," I said. "I think you have a bottle, too."

I offered her guacamole and chips before we started the mole. I gave her some beans on her tray, too.

"Okay, it's mole time. The chiles are ready to be pureed in the food processor, and the pork is ready to be fried."

"Thanks for waiting for me, Mia." She sat up in her bed.

The frying pork added another yummy aroma

to the kitchen. I pulled out the food processor and pureed the chiles. I poured them into a giant strainer to remove the seeds and skin.

"Oh, Mia, I don't know why you aren't using the powdered chiles," Mom broke in as the chiles slowly drained into the large glass bowl. "It's so much work for you to make the mole from scratch."

"I couldn't make your famous pork mole with chile powder," I said. "Besides, I need you to supervise me. I've never made it before."

"You've helped me, and all I can do now is supervise," Mom said, smiling.

"And I need your help," I said.

"I wasn't sure what you used for stock to thin the mole, so I boiled a few pork feet with garlic and onions. Will that work?"

"I usually use water," she said. "That sounds delicious, Mia. Good idea."

The pork was sizzling away, the chile nectar had almost completely strained and it was time to start the roux. "I'm going old school tonight, Mom, and using *manteca* for the mole instead of olive oil," I said.

"That's what I did for years, Mia, until I started

to have heart trouble. It's the way my mom taught me." She watched me gather the flour and lard to start the roux. "Make sure you use the cast iron skillet to fry your flour."

"Thanks for the reminder, Mom. I think Isabella keeps it in the garage."

I returned with cast iron skillet, put in about a cup of lard and watched it melt. "Do you think that's enough lard, Mom?" I asked.

"I think so, Mia. Make sure the lard is really hot before you pour in the flour," she said.

I began to pour in the flour, and mixed the oil and flour quickly. I turned down the burner.

"Is it too hot, Mia?" Mom said.

"I don't want to burn the roux, Mom. It will take longer with lower heat, but I've burnt it before so I need to go a little bit slower than you."

"I've never burnt it," Mom said.

"That's not surprising, Mom. You're a pro," I said. "I just wish you'd written this recipe down. It intimidates me. I think it's your hardest recipe."

"Oh, Mia, it's not that hard. You make chicken mole all the time, and you can make my pozole.

You're such a good cook, I know it's going to be delicious."

I reheated the rice and added onion and the remaining liquid ingredients. Every burner on Isabella's stove was on, and I was scrambling to stay calm. Just about then, my older sister Lena joined us for dinner. As guests arrived, I was concentrating on the brown roux, and Mom was concentrating on my mole making too — so much so that we barely acknowledged our guests.

Mom and I stayed in our mole-making zone. About 30 minutes in, I added more flour, knowing I needed to get the ratio of flour to *manteca* just right. I lifted the pan to show Mom the color. "What do you think, Mom, is it ready for me to add the chiles?"

"It looks perfect, Mia. Do you have a whisk nearby? You're going to need it as soon as you add the chiles and stock."

I searched Isabella's drawers for a whisk. "OK, all ready. Here we go."

I poured about two cups of the chile nectar into the roux, added about eight cups of the pork stock and whisked it quickly. I took momentary breaks from the mole to mix the pork that was golden brown and crunchy and almost ready for mole sauce. Alternating between the two items was nerve-racking.

"Mia, did you check the rice?" Mom said.

"Oh, Mom, thanks so much for reminding me," I said as I took the lid off the rice and saw that it was done, and now I had a free burner for the *comal* (heat tortillas).

"Do you need some help?" Isabella said as she came into the kitchen.

"Can you set out dinner plates, utensils, silverware, and I'll need you to start heating up tortillas in about 15 minutes."

"Oh, Mia, that looks so good. The red color is so rich and the thickness looks perfect," Mom said as I took the skillet of piping-hot mole sauce to the counter so she could get a good look.

"It needs salt, and is it cumin or cloves?" I asked my master chef.

"It takes cloves, Mia," Mom said.

I added about a teaspoon of crushed cloves and a little salt, mixed it well and took out a teaspoon. I blew on it to cool it down. "Okay, Mom, taste it and tell me if it needs anything else. The pork is going to be ready in about five minutes, so hopefully I'm close and we won't end up with mushy pork mole."

I watched as Mom took the spoonful in her mouth. I waited anxiously for her culinary opinions.

"Mia, it's perfect, just a little salt. It's so good. You're a better cook than me," she said.

"Oh please, Mom, not even close — stop. Besides, I wouldn't have been able to make this today without your help," I said.

"Well, I know that you are, Mia," she said.

"Thank you, Mom," I said as I poured the pork into a large colander to drain the fat. I gently scooped the crunchy pork into the mole sauce. Then I gave the signal to Isabella to heat the tortillas. We were five minutes and counting. I knew that if the pork stayed in there too long, it would be soft and mushy — not crunchy the way Mom liked it.

A few minutes later I gave Mom small servings of Peruvian refried beans, orange rice and crunchy pork mole and a flour tortilla.

"Here you go, Mom. Happy birthday."

I placed her plate on the tray.

Then the rest of our family lined up at the counter and started making their plates. I watched Mom as she carefully prepared her first bite. She used a small piece of her tortilla to scoop rice and mole, and placed it into her mouth. She closed her eyes as she chewed it. My heart was racing as I waited for her feedback.

"Oh, Mia, it's so delicious," she said, looking very emotional.

"You helped me," I said. "Thank you."

The rest of the family was happily eating their dinner, and even little Marisol was sitting in her high chair, eating beans and smiling after every bite. As I looked at them, this was it: nirvana for any home chef, everyone thoroughly enjoying my cooking. I savored this happy moment.

Mom finished all of her plate.

"Oh, Mia, it was all so good and you worked so hard, all day in the kitchen," she said.

"It's all good, Mom. I loved cooking for you, and I'm done for the evening."

The kids would do the dishes.

"Do you want us to move you to your chair for

a little while?" I said.

"Yes, Mia, I'd like that."

Isabella and I carefully moved Mom to her recliner. The conversation with everyone was lively, and Mom looked happy.

I snuck out to the garage to get her ice cream cake ready. I signaled Gabriel, and he turned off the lights as I entered the room carrying her ice cream cake with five small candles burning brightly. "Happy birthday to you…"

As I sat nearby and watched her enjoying her time with her family, talking, eating cake, opening presents and smiling, it occurred to me that my mother was capable of exiting her life with the same contentment that she'd lived. That's what she was teaching me all these years, to be content with every journey of my life.

Chapter Nine

Holiday Cooking

Celebrate your traditions with

joy and gratefulness.

This is truly one of the last gifts

you can give your loved ones.

And you might be surprised

by the connection and

love that you experience

during this final journey.

Day 325, Monday, Oct. 31, 2011

Jessie's Viking costume really came together, especially the horned hat. It had two large horns, and he was wearing a long brown jacket with a fur vest and large belt crisscrossed across his chest. He was also carrying 5 large rubber fish. We'd bought the hat, and I helped him put the rest of it together. I stood with him in our front yard as John took our pictures. Jessie had a huge smile and looked proud of his mostly homemade costume. John took a few pictures of him making silly faces and pretending to be ready to bite the life-size rubber fish.

It was the first year that Gabriel wasn't there for the Halloween celebration. One of the moms from our high school carpool had picked him up about 20 minutes earlier to drive him to school. He hadn't worn any sort of costume, which was understandable at his age — too old for Halloween costumes. They were growing up so fast.

We headed off to Jessie's Halloween parade at school, on the giant blacktop playground. There was loud Halloween music playing like "Monster Mash," and each class took its turn parading in a large circle. There were hundreds of parents, grandparents and family friends taking photos as the various witches, zombies, ghosts and monsters walked past us. I took tons of pictures and sent a few to Isabella so she could share them with Mom.

Almost the instant I was done with Halloween, when I left Jessie's school festivities to get to work, my thoughts turned to Thanksgiving. If this were a normal Thanksgiving like last year, we'd all go to Santa Maria for the long weekend, and I would cook with Mom.

I didn't know what to do. I knew this would be her last Thanksgiving. Did I really want to drag Gabriel, Jessie and John through that experience?

After dinner that night, I spoke to John, who suggested I ask the boys if they wanted to go. "If they don't, don't force it," he said.

I knew he was right. Mom's impending death was difficult for them to witness.

So, the next day I asked.

"I will go if I have to," Gabriel said.

"No," Jessie said.

"I understand why you don't want to go," I said. "It is okay for you to spend Thanksgiving with your father."

John was going to spend the holiday with his family in San Diego. I'd be spending Thanksgiving without John, Gabriel and Jessie, and more than ever I was torn and sad. I already regretted giving my sons the option to spend Thanksgiving with their father, but it was too late.

I broke the news to Mom. "I think it will be good for them to spend Thanksgiving with their father's family for a change," Mom said.

I knew she was disappointed. Like me, she was staying clear from conversational topics that could create conflict between us, and I was reminded again of how our relationship was changing. Any other time, Mom would have insisted that Gabriel and Jessie come with me. She knew it was in the divorce decree that the boys spend Thanksgiving with me, but this time she said nothing.

The next few weeks flew by, with work projects, preparation for Gabriel's holiday choral concerts and a couple more weekend trips to Mom's. I was tired, and Mom was progressively getting thinner and weaker, sleeping longer and was noticeably in pain, even though she didn't complain about it. I prayed that she'd hold on through the holidays.

Just one more holiday season is what I prayed for every day. Oh please, dear God, just one more Thanksgiving and Christmas with our sweet mama …

Day 348, Wednesday, Nov. 23, 2011

John was helping me pack the car for my solo Thanksgiving trip to Santa Maria. He was going to help Gabriel and Jessie finish packing as soon as they got home from school and then he'd be flying to San Diego.

"You really need to get on the road soon," he said. "The traffic's going to be terrible."

"Can you please remind them to take nice clothes for Thanksgiving dinner, too?" I said as I packed Sophia's bed and a few toys into the car.

John assured me he had it covered. He gave

me a huge hug and kiss goodbye.

Traffic was heavy, and it was slow going. When I stopped in King City, our usual Starbucks, gas and potty break, I saw lots of families traveling together. I longed for Gabriel, Jessie and John to be with me. Then it hit me that this would be the first year I wouldn't be with my sons on Thanksgiving. Had I made the right decision? I wasn't sure. My friends, sisters and John all thought so, but the one person whose opinion I valued the most was no longer my ultimate confidant.

I arrived in Santa Maria around 6:30 p.m. Isabella greeted me at the door and helped me unload the car. "Oh my goodness, Diana, did you bring your entire kitchen?"

"Dinner for tonight, Thanksgiving stuff and Mom's treats."

"Hello, beautiful Mama, how are you?" I said as I kissed Mom on her forehead.

"I was getting worried about you, Mia. Such a long drive for you today and all alone," she said, holding my hand and staring up at me from her recliner.

"I wasn't alone, Mom. I had the most traveled pup with me, little Princess Sophia," I said. "Are you hungry? I made some yummy clam chowder for dinner. I'm going to heat it up and toast some French bread in the oven."

"Make sure you put plenty of butter on the bread, Mia. Sometimes, you're stingy with the butter," she said in her master chef voice.

"I'll make sure I put lots of butter on it, but that means that you will be eating an entire piece with a little soup before you get any dessert," I said, smiling as I moved into the kitchen and started to unpack the food.

Mom watched intently the various containers I pulled from the large ice chest. "I love your clam chowder, Mia. I'll eat a little; just don't give me too much," Mom said. "OK, I saw the doughnuts, but did you make me some pumpkin squares?"

"You're too much, Mom," I said. "Eat your dinner first and then I'll show you your dessert options." As I said this, I poured the clam chowder into a large soup pot.

Next I buttered the French bread and put it into the oven for a few minutes. I put the rest of the food away for tomorrow's big Thanksgiving celebration. I served Mom a small bowl of soup and a slice of bread on her tray.

"Here's your dinner, sweet Mama." I placed the tray in her lap.

"Oh, Mia, it smells so good," she said as she lowered her head closer to the tray and took a deep breath to smell her dinner.

I returned to the kitchen and served myself some soup, then sat down next to Mom and ate with her.

"Your soup is so delicious, Mia," she said between spoonfuls. "It's far better than mine and even better than any I've ever had in any restaurants."

"And how about the bread. Does it have too much butter?" I said.

"It can never have too much butter," Mom said as she took a big bite of bread.

But I could see Mom struggled to eat it all. It was clear that she was forcing herself to finish her soup.

"Is the soup upsetting your stomach, Mom?" I said.

"No, Mia, it's so good. I just don't have much of an appetite tonight," she said.

"Thank you for trying to eat, Mom. You can stop anytime and I will still give you your dessert," I said.

"Nope, I'm going to finish it. I know it's good for me, Mia, and I have to keep eating."

In the kitchen, I washed the dishes. Then I called out the dessert options. "Lemon-filled doughnut. See's candy, Nuts and Chew. Pumpkin squares. Do you want a little of all three?"

"Oh, yum, Mia. I can have the doughnuts and See's candy tomorrow. Bring me a pumpkin square," she said. "I was hoping that you'd baked some for Thanksgiving."

"I had to make them for you, Mom. I know they're your favorite."

I took her a small piece with whipped cream, and then watched her enjoy every bite.

"Oh, Mia, I know this sounds terrible, but can

you put a few of your pumpkin squares in the freezer for me? There's going to be a lot of desserts tomorrow, and I want to make sure I get to enjoy these after Thanksgiving. I don't want everyone eating them all up." She had asked so shyly.

"Oh, Mom, you're absolutely terrible, not wanting to share your pumpkin squares," I mock-scolded her. "And yes, I will freeze them for you."

Our pleasant night had ended, and I got Mom ready for bed. The routine of helping her brush her teeth, cleaning her up a little, emptying her catheter and fixing her pillows was so familiar now, but I still despised how it made me feel. It was a constant reminder of Mom's fragile, painful existence, and it hurt to see her suffer. The sores on her face were worse than ever as I placed the mask on the oozing wounds. I blessed and kissed her forehead before getting ready for bed. I slept on the sectional next to her hospital bed. The loud sounds of Mom's oxygen compressor and the snoring dogs kept me awake most of the night. I could have joined the rest of the family upstairs, but I found it impossible to leave Mom alone.

"Ring, ring, ring..."

Mom was ringing her bell.

I jumped out of bed and raced to her side.

"Happy Thanksgiving, sweet Mama," I said as I removed her the mask and rewired her oxygen.

"Happy Thanksgiving, Mia." She took my hand. "You didn't sleep. You should really sleep upstairs tonight and get some rest. I'm worried about you."

"I'm fine, please don't worry. I love sleeping next to you," I said, but I quickly wanted to change the subject. "Do you want to watch the Thanksgiving parade?"

On the television, bands were marching down the streets. "When are you going to start the turkey?" Mom asked.

"Around 10 a.m." I was making Mom coffee. "I'm not putting the stuffing in it, so it will take about five hours to cook. Isabella wants to eat around 3 or 4."

"Oh, but it's so good in the turkey," Mom said.

"I don't know, Mom. All I remember about our big turkey-making adventures was how hard it was to get the stuffing out of the bird, always burning my hands, and the whole thing just stressing me out."

"Oh, Mia, how you love to exaggerate," Mom said, smiling.

"It's true," I said. "And remember we'd have like 40 people over. We'd make two giant turkeys, hams and all the fixings. We worked for days, the family ate in shifts and you and I ate last by ourselves. I didn't really like that, Mom. That's why I'm so fixated on all of us eating together."

"It was a lot of work, Mia, but everyone loved it," Mom said.

"Yes, they did, and I loved cooking with you, even it meant burning my hands off." And then I narrated for Mom how I was going to prepare it. I would brine it, then I planned to stuff it with celery, onions and garlic and coat it in herbs and butter. The extra touch was Grandma Amelia's Portuguese stuffing. "I'm going to cook it in the mini-Bundt muffins pan so the edges will get crunchy for you."

"That was one of the first recipes she ever taught me to make after your dad and I were married," Mom said. "The *linguica*, bacon, onions, peppers and celery give it a wonderful flavor. Your grandma was a very sweet lady."

I remembered her. "She used to make me coffee with about one tablespoon of coffee, three tablespoons of sugar and warm milk, and sit with me at her kitchen table and talk to me when we went to visit," I said. "I was only six when she died. It would have been nice to have spent more time with her."

"She had been suffering from stomach cancer for years, Mia," Mom said. "Her doctors didn't understand how she managed to live for so long."

I remembered when Grandma died. The whole family had gathered at her house at dinnertime, and she was in the hospital. "Daddy and I were sitting on a bench that faced her bedroom, and the door was open," I shared with Mom. "We saw lights appear from nowhere and twinkle above her bed. Daddy grabbed my hand, and we ran out the front door. Everyone else followed us outside, too. And as Daddy told everyone about what we'd seen, the phone rang in the house. He raced back into the house, and it was the hospital calling to tell us that she'd passed away."

I could see Mom remembered, too. "You were

so scared. Your dad saw so many unexplainable things, Mia. I think her soul came to say goodbye."

"Do you remember how he'd tell us about waking up with his knee hurting and proclaim that someone had died?" I said. "Or telling us about a dream where someone he knew came to visit him to say goodbye, and they were young again."

"And then we'd always get a phone call telling us that the person in the dream had died," Mom filled in. "The hurting knee proclamations always came true, too."

"I think Dad was kind of a portal for the dying," I said.

"I don't know what it was, Mia, but it was something."

In the kitchen, I got to work. I sized it all up. I'd made the stuffing at home, and the dessert was done. After I got the turkey in the oven, I would prepare mashed potatoes and gravy, and I thought I would serve spinach salad plus an appetizer. Isabella came into the kitchen and asked if she could help. It was basically the same menu that Mom and I had made together for years. The only new additions were the spinach salad and pumpkin squares that I had added after I went to college.

"Aren't we having rolls with butter, too? And you made pumpkin squares, but what about pie?" Mom asked from her hospital bed.

"Yes, Mom, we're having rolls, and Joyce's family is bringing pies." I turned to Isabella. "Clearly, Mom will be supervising us today," I said with a smile. "Can you arrange a couple of folding tables next to Mom's recliner so we can all eat together?"

Most years we celebrated Thanksgiving in Isabella's garage. We'd spend hours decorating it with cascading strings of lights, flowers, white linen tablecloths and beautiful place cards, but this year would be different. We passed a knowing look between us. It would be impossible for us to get Mom into the garage, and perhaps too cold for her.

"I'd like to wear a dress today," Mom said. "Can one of you girls help me get dressed?"

Isabella volunteered. "Do you know what dress you want to wear?"

"Yes, I have a brown one with bright orange,

green and yellow flowers," Mom said.

For most of a year, she hadn't worn anything but nightgowns.

Isabella spent the next hour getting Mom ready for our big Thanksgiving celebration, and I started working on dinner. My older sister had provided a fresh, grain-fed organic turkey. I had brined it the night before. I took it out of the refrigerator and stuffed it with garlic, onions, celery and oranges and covered it with an herbed olive oil paste. Mom looked at me stuffing the bird with veggies and shook her head disapprovingly. I knew she was teasing me, and I loved having her nearby to watch and provide commentary.

I explained: "My old roommate, who studied at the San Francisco Culinary Institute, gave me this recipe. It's not yours, but I promise that it will be delicious."

The spinach salad came next. It was Mom's favorite salad. Years ago, when I was in college and a caregiver for a lovely woman, she had taught me the recipe. Since then, it had become our Thanksgiving menu tradition. It called for bacon, hard-boiled eggs, green onions, spinach, shredded almonds, spinach and balsamic dressing. To get it started, I fried the bacon and boiled the eggs. The bacon aroma quickly drew Sophia and Gigi into the kitchen, where they trained their sad puppy eyes on me with the hope of scoring a bite. They both knew me too well. I gave in to their cuteness.

Next, I peeled potatoes. I sliced them and placed them in a tall soup pot with a little fresh lemon and salt. I made salad dressing while the eggs cooled, then sliced green onions and mushrooms.

Isabella had finished dressing Mom in her hospital bed.

"Wow! You look beautiful, Mom."

"Is the headband too much?" Mom pointed to her hair.

"It's perfect, Mom," I said. "It matches your cute dress."

"The turkey smells good, Mia. Have you checked it?" she said.

"I'll check it in about an hour to see how fast it's cooking," I said. "I don't need to baste it because of how I used the olive oil paste. All the veggies inside keep it moist. It usually cooks super-fast this way."

"I asked Isabella to make me some compotes," Mom said, referring to our sweet yam recipe. It was her way of telling me that the kitchen would be invaded soon.

"That's good, Mom. I know how much you love them. I'm not a big fan, and I always forget to add them to our menu."

"I know," she said.

"I do have a surprise for you, though. I'm making my spinach sausage dip in the giant sourdough bread. It's been years since I made it for you. It's basically going to be your lunch, and I guess you'll want a lemon doughnut for dessert."

"I love spinach dip, Mia."

There, I had made her smile.

The parade was over, and Mom settled in for a nap. The rest of the family was upstairs, and I watched her sleep in her pretty dress. To my surprise I wasn't melancholy about today. I truly felt joyful to be here cooking one last Thanksgiving dinner for her. I knew she was happy to watch me cook, be my guest and take less of a supervisory role. I felt somehow she had passed the cooking baton to me. Something had shifted. She was letting go.

Isabella and her daughters had arranged the tables in an L shape so that Mom's recliner was at the top of the L and we could all sit together. She'd covered the tables with brightly colored fall tablecloths and flowers and while modest if compared to previous years, it was perfect.

The delicious aromas of the turkey and ham filled the house. I prepared Mom a small plate with sourdough bread and spinach dip. Watching her take a bite flooded me with memories. I saw her younger, healthier, laughing and smiling while we ate the scrumptious dip together. I didn't even remember where I'd gotten the original recipe, and of course I'd updated it over the years. The primary ingredients included spinach, mushrooms, Italian sausage, cream cheese, caramelized onions, Parmesan and Asiago cheese.

Dinner wouldn't be completely ready for about another hour, so I took the opportunity to organize a small photo shoot with Mom and all her guests. Isabella helped me move her from her chair to the sofa. One by one they sat next to Mom for pictures. Everyone was pleasant and cooperative. And not one of the household teenagers gave me any grief about the photo shoot with their beloved grandmother. All of us knew that we'd be very grateful for these photos soon.

The final countdown was chaotic. Potatoes were mashed, corn was buttered, peas were boiled, gravy was warmed, salad was tossed, rolls were heated and at last, the turkey and ham were carved. A crew of line cooks assembled to help me as my master chef watched from her chair. Timing a dinner with such a large menu was tricky — Mom had taught me that a long time ago. All the side dishes needed to stay hot, and the salad couldn't get soggy. I wanted it to be just perfect. It was a task of mammoth proportions.

Thankfully, there were no kitchen catastrophes. Even the individual stuffing servings popped out of the miniature Bundt pan easily and looked stunning, with golden brown edges and an adorable serving size.

The family lined up to make their plates. I plated Mom's dinner with a little bit of everything and took it to her. With each scoop — mashed potatoes, corn, peas, stuffing, turkey, ham and spinach salad — I was increasingly filled with emotion. I knew I would never make her another Thanksgiving plate. Looking at the colorful array of foods and flavors on the plate, I had to keep reminding myself to be grateful for this moment.

Marisol's high chair was directly across from Mom. She was eating mashed potatoes with both hands and had smeared them all over her face. Mom was watching her adoringly and smiling. Looking around at everyone as we ate, I saw lively, joyful faces and I was truly happy. After eating, we sat for a long while, reminisced and shared funny stories, which seemed to primarily focus on my cooking disasters. Pumpkin pies had been the subject of repeated disasters during a stretch of a few years. One year I forgot to add sugar. The second year I used salt instead of sugar. The third year I removed the pies from the oven and placed them on the stove burners, and one pie burned. These sequential pumpkin pie tragedies had led me to retire as a pumpkin pie baker, which led to pumpkin squares, a recipe that a co-worker had shared at a holiday potluck. Mom had approved of the menu update. All in all, it was a lovely dinner and it was clear that no one wanted it to end.

"This was the best Thanksgiving ever," Mom said.

As I took her plate, I struggled to hold back my tears.

"The food was amazing," she continued. "You're a much better cook than me."

"I don't agree with you, Mom, but thank you." I brimmed with gratitude for this moment.

I snuck out of the house at 4:30 a.m. for a little Black Friday shopping. It was my annual tradition and I was hoping it would help me get into the holiday spirit. It was the first time that I ever looked at other shoppers and wondered if they too were buying gifts for a dying loved one. Needless to say my attempts to jump-start my holiday cheer failed. But I did manage to buy a few comfort gifts for Mom; soft nightgowns, sheets and fragrant lotions. I wouldn't need to make her another calendar until February.

By Saturday, I was stiff and creaking from sleeping on a couch. I woke up around 5 a.m., terribly missing my sons and John. I knew being with Mom right now was a gift, but I also longed for them. I decided to go home a day early and beat the traffic. I would be able to decorate our house for Christmas before going back to work on Monday. The morning brought confusion and regret about where to be. Who needed me more? Who was my first priority? Was I balancing the needs of my sons and my mother? I was torn.

"Ring, ring, ring…"

I was snapped out of my pity party.

"Good morning, beautiful," I said as I started to rewire her mask and oxygen.

"Look at you, Mia." She took my hand and looked sadly up at me. "The circles under your eyes are bigger than ever."

"That's probably just smeared mascara."

"I have to worry about you, Mia. Look all the driving you're doing, not sleeping, away from the boys. I've been thinking, and I don't want you coming to see me so much, Mia. There are tons of leftovers in the freezer, and you need to rest and spend time with your sons. Now that I'm here with Isabella, it's easier on her, and I know she'll understand if you slow down a little on visiting me. Don't get me wrong, Mia, I love seeing you. But this is far too much for you."

"I love coming to see you, Mom. And seriously, I'm fine. John is helping me out so much with Gabriel and Jessie. But I'll think about it."

Standing in the kitchen as I brewed the coffee, I was blown away by Mom's intuition. Had she been eavesdropping on my morning thoughts? Now I had permission to slow down.

When I explained to Mom that I would leave about 1 p.m. to get a jump on Christmas decorations and laundry, she understood. "Do you think you can help Isabella get me into my wheelchair today before you leave? I'd like to sit outside on the patio. It's a gorgeous day, and I'd love to sit in the sun for a little while."

It wasn't easy to maneuver Mom into the wheelchair, but Isabella and I managed it. Even though Mom was weak and thin, it was still very hard for us to lift her.

Isabella found Mom a gigantic straw hat, and we covered her with a lightweight pink blanket. To wheel Mom outside, we had to lift the chair over the sliding glass door molding and slightly angle the chair. Once outside, I noticed it was sunny and in the mid-70s, with no wind. We parked her wheelchair in the sunshine. Perfection.

"Oh, Mia, it feels so good." Mom squinted a little from the brightness. She began to look around Isabella's patio. The water fountain and slowly moving wind chimes created a very tranquil space. Isabella and I sat down on patio chairs next to Mom. Mom began to nod off and catch a little nap. She looked so small in her wheelchair and giant straw hat, hunched over a little. She looked old, tired and weak, and it was clear that her body was simply worn out. And then I noticed that she wasn't napping. Her head was bobbing a little from side to side.

"I think she's crying," I whispered to Isabella.

"Mom, are you okay?" Isabella said in a loud, clear voice.

"It's all gone by way too fast." Mom raised her head, and I could see tears running down her face.

"These 84 years just flew by, and I don't want to leave you two. You must cherish your lives, because before you know it, it will be over."

I could see her lips were trembling, and her face was a mask of agony.

"You've been the best mother."

I stood up to hug her. Now tears were streaming down my face.

Isabella tried to console her, too. I knew Mom was speaking, but I couldn't comprehend her words. My heart broke with the knowledge that I couldn't undo this; I couldn't fix this for her. She was leaving us, and she didn't want to go.

Eventually, Mom stopped crying and quietly fell asleep again. Witnessing her sadness, I went over the emotional edge.

"I don't know if I can keep coming every weekend, Sis," I said after a while. "I'm exhausted. I miss my sons and John. This has gone on for almost 12 months. Mom's a fighter, and there is no telling how much longer she can continue." I looked over to Mom as she slept.

"It's okay, Diana," Isabella said. "It's easier now

that Mom is here. I don't know how you've done this. Mom has been so worried about your coming every weekend."

"I'm going to slow down a little in December. Gabriel has several concerts, Jessie has a Christmas pageant, and I can't miss them." I still felt conflicted.

"I understand, Diana."

"I don't know how you do this every day, Isabella," I said. "It's easier for me. I just have to be strong in front of her on the weekends. I don't know what we'd do without you." I reached out to hug her.

When Mom woke from her nap, she was clearly very depressed. I helped Isabella get Mom's wheelchair back inside. I quickly packed up my car, then took Sophia and Gigi on a short walk. It was lunchtime, and I was eager to get on the road.

I took Mom's hand. "I'm going home, beautiful Mama."

She took my hand. "It was so good to see you, Mia."

"I'll call you when I get home." I kissed her forehead, then blessed her.

By the time I reached the first stoplight, tears

were streaming down my face. The image of my sick, sad, broken mama was imprinted on my brain. It was all I could see and hear. Life seemed so cruel. Why do we have to grow old and leave the ones we love? I knew I had to get it together, but for now, with just me and Sophia and the 101, I just let the tears roll.

Day 381, Monday, Dec. 26, 2011

Between Thanksgiving and Christmas, I went only twice to see Mom. I spent more time with my sons and John. I'd decorated our house with Christmas lights and a beautiful tree, even made a gingerbread house with Jessie. I'd gone to every one of Gabriel's concerts and Jessie's Christmas pageant. "It's all gone by way too fast," Mom had said. Those words had echoed in my heart this past month. They had shifted to help me see that Gabriel and Jessie needed me, too. It was good to spend more time with my beautiful sons.

We all spent a wonderful Christmas Eve and Christmas morning together in our home. For

Christmas Eve dinner, I made Mom's pozole. Plenty was left over, so I planned to take it to Santa Maria. On Christmas morning, I made Gabriel, Jessie and John their favorite breakfast, *chorizo* y *papas sopitas*. My sons spent the rest of the day with their father, then John and I had a nice dinner with friends.

The day after Christmas, Gabriel and Jessie came home so we could pack for Santa Maria to celebrate Christmas with Mom. I packed up the pozole and See's candy. As usual, we stopped for Krispy Kreme doughnuts. All of her favorites.

My sons were usually thrilled to be going to Santa Maria to visit their cousins and see their grandmother, but not today. I noticed they were very subdued as we drove down the 101.

When we stopped in King City for gas, Starbucks and breakfast, it occurred to me to speak to Gabriel and Jessie about Mom's continued decline, but I decided against it. They would see her soon enough.

But the question came as we got back on the highway.

"Mom, does she look a lot worse than when we

celebrated her birthday?"

Gabriel sounded nervous.

"Yes, Gabriel," I said. "She's lost more weight and she coughs more. But she will be so happy to see you."

There were no follow-up questions. Gabriel quietly looked out the window as we approached Santa Maria. I longed for words to help him feel better, but none came.

When we saw her, she was thinner than ever. My first thought was that my attempts to make her yummy food and keep her from losing more weight were failing. But really, I didn't understand how she had managed to hold on this long. I wasn't alone in this. No one understood: Not her hospice nurses, not my sister. It couldn't be explained.

"You've grown more since the last time I saw you, Gabriel," Mom said. "You're so handsome."

I felt grateful for Mom's big smile.

As Jessie leaned in to kiss his grandma, it hit me. *My giant teenage sons look like small, frightened boys.* I could feel their hurt as I watched them trying their best to converse with their frail grandmother.

Gabriel stood closest to her with Jessie standing farther back, almost unable to look at her. He hadn't seen her since the summer, and that was maybe 20 pounds ago. I knew this was hard for my sons, and I was proud of them.

Going to visit Mom the day after Christmas had been our routine for years. We'd anxiously sit together as soon as we arrived to open presents. We'd sort all the gifts, pick numbers and rotate through everyone until all packages were opened and we were all thrilled.

This time we didn't open gifts right away. We gathered around her and opened a few gifts. This was a far cry from previous Christmas holidays, which often lasted a few hours, full of gifts and banter. There were just two rounds this time. Isabella and I had done very little Christmas shopping this year, and Mom had done none. She gave the boys money. We gave Mom a few comfy nightgowns, sheets, perfume, candy and cashews — and no calendar. And she didn't mention it. I was grateful for that. Gabriel and Jessie were appreciative for their small gifts and money, and thankfully didn't complain or seem disappointed. Isabella's family was gracious, too. Everyone knew that this was Mom's last Christmas, and they were on good behavior.

Throughout this scene, little Marisol crawled around trying to get into the presents spread on the floor. I made a mental note that Marisol was a constant reminder of the circle of life. She was an adorable, happy, giggling baby, and Mom adored her.

After we opened gifts, everyone went upstairs and Mom and I were left alone with Gigi and Sophia. "Are you hungry, Mom? I brought pozole and tamales," I said.

"Where do you get the tamales?" Mom asked.

"From our little spot in San Jose. They're pretty good. Not as good as yours, because no one makes them as good as you." I looked up at her and smiled.

"We've made thousands of tamales together." Mom's eyes met mine. "But our tamale-making days are over."

"I don't think I'll ever be able to make them without you. I'm too scared," I said. "You're the master tamale maker, and I'd never get the *masa* right."

"I know you can do it, Mia. I hope you will try

someday." Mom seemed to think some more about this. "It would be a shame for your grandmother's tamale recipe to be lost forever."

Then her thoughts seemed to go in another direction. Her tone brightened. "I really love that picture you took of me and Marisol, Mia. Do you think we can use it on my headstone?"

I played this straight, just answering the question. "I don't think so, Mom. It's a great photo, but there's already a picture of you and Daddy on your headstone."

"Oh, that's right. I forgot."

The next words she spoke were in a stronger tone. "I think he's forgotten me."

"Who's forgotten you?" I was almost afraid to ask.

"Jesus! He's forgotten me. He made me come back, I got to meet Marisol, and now I think he's forgotten me," she said.

"Oh, Mom, I'm sure he hasn't forgotten you." Right at this moment, I longed for a personal dialogue writer, someone who could give me powerful words of wisdom that I could speak to my mother.

Mom was quiet and looked sad.

"Mom, you need to go," I said softly, directly into her good ear. "We will be okay. You've held on long enough. You've been the best mother ever, but please don't hang on any longer because of me. I know this isn't easy for you."

"Thank you, Mia." Tears filled her eyes as she turned to look deeply into mine. "I couldn't have asked for a better daughter."

We both sat there quietly. There was a knowing: We had just said our final goodbyes and openly acknowledged that our road together was ending.

Mom was the first to break the silence. "Do you really think that heaven exists?"

"I do, Mom, with all my heart," I said boldly, trying to sound confident through my tears. "And as I've told you before, I'm fairly sure that you've got a giant corner suite with an ocean view waiting for you."

"I'm not scared to die, Mia. I just really don't want to leave you girls. I think there is a heaven too, but I'm not sure that my little life has earned me a corner suite like you say. I haven't done anything extraordinary with my life. I was just a housewife."

"I don't think it has anything to do with our careers or worldly accomplishments, Mom. I think it has more to do with what kind of people we are, and you're an amazing person, filled with love and the exceptional ability to forgive — and I think that's what counts. Look how many people consider you to be their mother. There's about 15 people who call you Mom, and you gave birth to only three of us. Your legacy is your faith, and all the love you've given us." I was starting to convince myself that what awaited her was truly spectacular. "And we haven't always been easy to love."

Mom sat quietly again. I sat there wishing for more words that could help convey my love. I knew this was the last time we'd ever speak to each other like this.

A few minutes later she told me that she was tired, and I put her back to bed and rewired her mask oxygen so she could sleep. The sores around the mask were worse than they'd ever been, oozing pus and blood. I tried to place her mask on her face as gently as possible. It took me awhile to adjust her pillows, too. She had a couple of large bedsores on her tailbone that were also oozing pus and smelled like rotting flesh. I nearly called Isabella to help me, but finally managed to find a position where Mom said she didn't hurt. I covered her with blankets for her nap.

I sat there with her instead of going upstairs with the rest of the family. My mind raced as I watched her labored breathing and her face grimace with pain as she slept. "Oh, please, take her soon, dear God," I prayed. Tears streamed down my cheeks as I looked into her face.

I decided to make Mom some simple chicken soup. It would be easier for her to eat and better for her health. Isabella came down later and couldn't believe I was making chicken soup when there were tamales and pozole.

"I told Mom it was okay for her to go," I said.

I could see Isabella understood me, but I wanted it to be clear: "You need to do the same."

Mom was suffering too much.

Isabella said she would tell her, and tell her soon.

Chapter Ten

Daddy Takes Her Home

Death comes for her.

My journey has ended.

I am filled with grief, sorrow and loss.

But I turn my thoughts to focus

on all the joy and love I gave her.

She is free of pain.

She is home.

I did my best.

Day 397, Wednesday, Jan. 11, 2012

I felt extremely guilty as I picked up my phone to call Isabella. I knew she was going to be disappointed. "Hi, Sis. I'm not coming down this weekend. John's father is coming to visit. There are leftovers in the freezer for Mom to eat, including some yummy chicken soup," I blurted out, feeling my heart race.

"It's okay, Sis. You need to stay home and visit with him. I understand," she said, but I heard the disappointment in her voice.

"May I speak to Mom?" I asked.

After a few minutes, I heard Mom's voice, struggling between shallow breaths. "Hi, Mia, how are you?" She was too weak to hold her telephone anymore, so I knew Isabella held it next to her ear.

"Hello, beautiful. I'm good," I said. "I am not coming down to visit you this weekend. John's father is coming to visit us. I'm sorry."

"Don't you worry, Mia," she said, trying to hold off a coughing attack. "I will be fine and you need to stay home and visit, and hopefully you will get some rest too. I'm worried about you."

Somehow this made me feel worse, that she understood my predicament of wanting to be in two places at the same time. "I'm making him your yummy Sonora beef enchiladas," I offered. "John sure loves them, Mom. I'll save you some. I'm so grateful that you taught me the recipe."

"I love those enchiladas, too, and I can't wait," she said and then a horrible coughing spell came upon her and she had to hang up. Twenty minutes later I called Isabella back to make sure that Mom was okay. Isabella assured me that she was fine and resting. And although neither of us said it out loud, Mom's ability to breathe was declining. We both knew it.

I made Mom's Sonora enchiladas Thursday night. As I fried the hamburger, grated the cheese and prepared the counter to work, memories of cooking with Mom flooded me. We had made thousands of enchiladas for parties, fundraisers and funerals. I had watched so many friends and family's faces fill with joy as they took their first bites of her enchiladas. And my dad eating them with boiled, salted potatoes. He ate potatoes with everything and Mom never cared that he wouldn't eat her beloved orange rice. I felt grateful for all those memories and terribly sad that there would be no more.

John's father loved our celebratory dinner of Spicy Sonora Enchiladas, orange rice, beans and guacamole. I tried to be present with my sons, John and his father during our festive dinner Friday night and again Saturday, but it was a struggle.

As hard as I tried, my thoughts eventually went to Mom, always cold now, with severe coughing spells and in constant pain. Oh, how I wished for a magic wand to fix all her booboos and cook some huge feast with her.

Day 397, Sunday, Jan. 15, 2012

On Sunday, I went about my normal household activities and didn't call Mom until late in the afternoon. The 49ers were playing.

When I called Isabella, she said, "She's

wearing her mask right now." I heard the anxiety in her voice. "She can't breathe."

But I wanted more than anything to speak with Mom. I insisted.

"I don't think she can speak to you, Sis," Isabella said in a sad voice. "She's not doing well at all."

"I'll be there soon, Sis. Just need to pack a few things." My heart was racing. "Please tell Mom I'm on my way." The familiar tears sprang to my eyes.

I walked into the den to speak to John. "I need to go to Santa Maria right now, John. Mom's not doing well." I heard my words come slowly, as if they could hold back tears.

John noticed my face and gave me a big hug. "Okay, Babe, do what you need to do. I've got this. The boys and my dad will be fine."

I packed my bag quickly, put the enchiladas in a small ice chest, and Sophia and I started our four-hour drive to Santa Maria. It was my 39th trip in 13 months. My continual prayer was: Oh, God, please help me to ease her fears about going to heaven.

The drive was easy. Highway 101 and I were

bonded after all my drives to Santa Maria, and there wasn't much traffic on a Sunday night. The rollercoaster of Mom's condition had taken its toll on all of us. My sons were having a hard time accepting that she was dying and didn't understand why I had to go if I'd agreed to stay home for the weekend. I knew that Mom's tenaciousness gave others false hope.

Arriving in Santa Maria just a few minutes before 9 p.m., I was shocked when I saw Mom and Isabella. Mom was in a terrible state. Isabella was standing near her hospital bed, leaning over Mom's body and speaking to her calmly as Mom thrashed her head back and forth and violently waved her left arm. Mom was wearing her mask and didn't notice my arrival immediately.

Isabella looked exhausted and frightened. "I'm glad you're here," she said as Mom held onto her hand tightly and didn't let her go, and Isabella hugged me with one arm.

I had to be strong. I summoned every bit of strength I had left in me, gently took Mom's other hand and smiled at her. She looked surprised to see me. "I heard you weren't behaving, so I had to come and see if I could bribe you with some enchiladas and lemon-filled doughnuts," I said loudly so she could hear me over the noise of her mask and oxygen tank.

I held her hand, gently moved her bangs off her forehead and lightly kissed her. I showed her the ice chest with her enchiladas and her box of Krispy Kremes.

"I'm not misbehaving," she said, struggling to speak through the mask.

"I heard differently. All you need is some good food and you'll be better," I said cheerfully as I signaled my sister to peel Mom's clenched hand from hers.

Isabella ran out of the room in tears. Mom's gaze followed Isabella down the hallway, and I explained that Isabella needed to rest and would be back later. Mom didn't want to be alone for even a second now. She always wanted Isabella with her.

Mom looked up at me with a little twinkle in her eye. "Can I have half a lemon doughnut before I eat dinner? And don't tell your sister."

"I'll let you have a doughnut, Mom." I smiled.

I started the process of removing her mask

and rewiring her oxygen nasal cannula. She grimaced with pain as I lifted it off her face. The sores on the bridge of her nose and cheeks were noticeably bigger, and blood and pus were oozing from them again.

Countless attempts to treat them over Mom's long illness had all failed. I was losing my ability to hold it together. The heartbreak of witnessing her suffer month after month welled up inside me, and it felt like I had a giant hairball stuck in the back of my throat as I struggled to breathe. I ran to the kitchen and sipped water as I tried to clear my throat. I prayed to the Virgen de Guadalupe and told myself, "Be strong, Mom's here and she needs you."

I returned to her side and raised the bed up slowly. I pulled her gently forward as I arranged the pillows behind her head. She needed to be more upright so she wouldn't choke as she ate.

I saw her try to pick up the doughnut and realized that she wasn't able to feed herself anymore. I quickly cut a small piece and placed it in her mouth. She looked up at me. "This is so good. I love lemon doughnuts. Thank you, Mia." I continued to feed her, trying to hold back my tears as she struggled to chew and started coughing a few times. I gave her a few sips of milk and she finished the doughnut.

"Do you want an enchilada and a little rice now? You promised to eat, if I gave you a doughnut," I said as I gently cleaned her face and hands with a warm cloth.

"I'm too full right now. I'll eat later, I promise. Just stay here and tell me about your weekend," she said. I held her hand, sat next to her bed and told her about Gabriel, Jesse, John and the mundane events of our daily life. She listened to me as she always had, making me feel like I was the most important person in her whole world.

"You girls, you are so good to me. I'm so lucky. You are the best daughters ever," she said sadly.

"We had a good teacher," I replied.

She said this all the time now. And told everyone who came to visit her. This was all she could give us now. No more homemade tortillas, leftover food to take home, lemons and oranges from her trees. All she could give us now were warm compliments of gratitude, and I was grateful that she had the grace to tell us often.

Sophia jumped up on my lap. I picked her up and held her over Mom's torso. Mom sweetly patted her head and told her she was a good girl. Little Gigi was next. I picked her up and Mom did the same, petting her head and speaking sweet words of gratitude to her beloved dog. "They're such loving dogs," she said with a gentle smile, and looked away from Gigi sadly.

She managed to eat about half of an enchilada and a few spoons of rice about an hour later. I cut her food up and fed her slowly.

"It's so good, Mia, but I'm sorry, I'm just too full and I can't eat anymore," she said.

"Do you want me to get you ready for bed?" I removed her dinner plate from her bed tray.

"Yes, I'm tired."

I gently washed her face with a warm cloth, brushed her teeth, emptied her catheter and arranged her pillows. I ran up the stairs to ask Isabella about Mom's bedtime meds.

It was late, so I wasn't sure what Mom still

needed. "I'm sorry for leaving you alone with Mom," she said sitting up in her bed.

"No need to apologize," I replied. "I get it. It's very hard to watch our pillar of strength crumble in front of us while we helplessly stand by and witness it."

Isabella hugged me. "Yes, it is."

Isabella decided to come downstairs with me, gave Mom her nightly meds and asked me to help her roll Mom to one side so Isabella could treat Mom's bedsores. I gasped when I saw them. Poor Mom had two huge oozing sores in the crack of her butt cheeks. Mom screamed in pain as Isabella cleaned and treated them with ointment. My sister went on to explain to me that this was the latest of my mother's many complications.

"Will they get better?" I asked as she got Mom some more pain medication.

"I don't know," she whispered. "Mom can't breathe if she lays on her side, and they most likely won't heal if she lies on them all the time."

What I heard between the words was that Mom's pain levels were increasing.

I thanked Isabella for helping me and told her to go back to bed. "I will get Mom's mask on."

"No more mask," Mom gasped.

"If you don't wear your mask, it will be hard for you to breathe and your carbon dioxide levels will get too high, Mom," replied Isabella in her official stern RN voice.

"No mask," Mom repeated.

"If that's what you want, Mom, then no mask tonight," I said.

Isabella gave me a sad, knowing look, kissed Mom goodnight, blessed her and went upstairs.

"Are you mad at me for not wearing my mask tonight?" Mom said as I arranged her bedding and pillows.

"No, Mom, I'm not mad at you. How could I be? I know it hurts you. I just don't want you to suffer anymore," I said.

"Are you saying that you want me to die?" she asked.

"Mom, you know I don't want you to die, but I know this isn't easy for you, and I don't want you to keep hanging on for us. You're going straight to heaven, to that corner suite with an ocean view." Tears rolled down my face now.

"Do you really think it's beautiful?" she said. "Heaven, I mean."

"Yes, Mom, I think it is more beautiful than we can even imagine, and you'll be reunited with all your family and still be able to keep an eye on us, too." I heard the sincere conviction in my voice.

"I sure hope you're right," she said.

"I am and you know I am, Mom. I love you. You've been the best mom ever. Thank you." I kissed her forehead, blessed her and tucked her in.

I sat next to her for about 30 minutes and watched her as she fell asleep. Her breathing was shallow, but she looked peaceful. I turned on the baby monitor and quietly went upstairs to check on Isabella.

She was a wreck. And while it was hard for me, I knew it was harder for Isabella as Mom's primary caregiver. She went on to tell me that Mom had a terrible Saturday night, and she'd been up with her most of the night. She also explained that Mom might slip into a coma without her mask and never wake up again. I knew this, and I tried to help her understand that Mom was holding on for us. We needed to give her permission to leave. She wasn't going anywhere until we both did so.

We ran down the stairs as we heard Mom screaming through the baby monitor. She was crying and completely hysterical. We tried to speak to her, held her hands, rubbed her forehead, but she was unresponsive to our voices and touch. Mom was in her own world, frightened and having endless conversations with herself and others we couldn't see.

It was one of the longest, most painful nights of our lives. Isabella was convinced that Mom was delusional from her elevated carbon dioxide levels. We tried to put her mask on at some point, but she fought us and I made us stop trying.

After a few hours, Mom calmed down. Then she started having animated conversations with dead relatives we couldn't see. I tried to join in the conversation, but she ignored my questions about my dead aunts and cousins. She finally fell asleep about 4 a.m. Sophia and I slept on the cozy tan recliner next to her, and I was never more grateful to be able to sleep an arm's length from my sweet mama.

The next morning, she could barely speak. I convinced Isabella that it was time to call our large extended family. It was time for everyone to say goodbye. At first Isabella resisted and thought Mom might rebound again. I had to explain that it was unlikely now that Mom was refusing to wear her mask. She finally agreed, and I made the calls to Mom's nieces, nephews, other children and close friends.

The first relatives arrived about 30 minutes after my call. Mom greeted everyone in her nightgown, from her hospital bed, her hair a mess — but her thin body still able to illuminate love and grace. Mom was happy to see everyone and was full of smiles. And while she struggled to speak, she did manage to tell me to make them coffee.

Her relatives looked at her softly, and some took her hand as they said their heartfelt goodbyes. She hugged them all and told them she loved them and they had been a good family. I knew there had been tension with some of the family members who came to visit, and some of them hadn't visited Mom in years, but she greeted them all with gratefulness, forgiveness and love.

The parade of relatives lasted most of the day. Isabella struggled with this, but I kept reminding her that it was making Mom happy. These people deserved an opportunity to say goodbye too. This wasn't about us — it was about Rose.

Late that afternoon, our cousin, Maria and her husband, Carlos, were the last to visit. Maria was Mom's favorite niece and lifetime best friend. Mom managed to sit up in bed and have a complete conversation with Maria for about 20 minutes. She was lucid and so happy to chat with Maria. Isabella and I were in shock.

Maria scolded us as she left the house for scaring her. It was clear that Mom was fine and not going anywhere soon, and she didn't understand why we had alerted the entire family. We tried to explain that she hadn't been able to speak clearly since the night before until her visit. Maria dismissed us and told us to not be such worrywarts.

Maria left, and we returned to our mother's side. Once again she was struggling to speak and breathe. Reluctantly, I packed, as I had to return to northern California and go to work Tuesday. I said goodbye to Mom and Isabella, and Sophia and I started our drive home Monday night. I cried most of the way. I wondered if I would ever see Mom alive again.

I got home about 10 p.m. and told John about Mom's condition. I was going back Thursday afternoon as soon as an important work meeting ended. Gabriel overheard me and announced he was coming with me. John would join us Friday after work. Jessie didn't want to come, and I decided not to force him.

Day 401, Thursday, Jan. 19, 2012 — My 40th Visit

When Isabella met me at the door, I saw the fear on her face. Mom was worse.

"I'm so glad you're here, Sis," she said. "The priest just left. She's been calling out for you."

I took a deep breath as I walked into the great room to greet Mom. My heart sank. It had been only two days, but it might as well have been a year. I reached down to hug her, and she was twisted into a fetal position and unable to hug me back. I heard her softly try to say my name as I kissed her forehead and gently swept her hair back. Her eyes pierced through me as I felt her unleash her love toward me. Her mouth stayed slightly open, and as if Isabella guessed my question, she said softly, "I think she had a mild stroke."

Gabriel reached down to hug his grandmother. I knew he was fighting back tears, and I was so grateful that he'd decided to come.

I tried to hold Mom's hands as I stood by her hospital bed, but they were clenched. Mom's exit had been slow and challenging to witness, and now more than ever I prayed for her to go home quickly to be free of pain and suffering. Mom kept looking at me as she struggled to breathe — no more mask for her, but she still wore her oxygen. Her carbon dioxide levels must be so high now, poisoning her. She was thrashing as she tried to speak to me, but I couldn't understand her. I asked Isabella if she knew what Mom needed. She shook her head. "No, and I don't know how much she can really hear us now, Diana."

I tried listening to her again and although I couldn't understand her, I instinctively knew what she wanted. When she had learned that she was dying 13 months earlier, she was determined to be alive for the birth of her first great-granddaughter, Marisol, and now in her final moments, she wanted to see her one last time.

"Mom, I'll be right back. I think I know what you want."

Marisol was in the next room with her mama and still awake. I returned to Mom with bright-eyed, 10-month-old Marisol a few minutes later. I placed Marisol on the front right side of Mom's bed and held her hands as she stood near Mom's waist. Mom tried to reach out and touch her, and was calm. Marisol spoke to her in her garbled babbles and coos. I joyfully watched Mom as she found happiness even in these final moments of life!

The rest of my family gathered around her bed. I moved Marisol closer as she reached out with her tiny hand to touch her great-grandma's cheek. We continued this until Mom fell asleep.

I slept next to Mom — just as I had for my last 39 visits — on the recliner. She was peaceful all night. Her oxygen tank was running and loud as always, but I didn't hear her coughing, nor did she call out to me — and I knew she could no longer ring her little bell. I made Isabella turn off the baby monitor so she could rest. It had been a long week for her. I kept waking up and checking on Mom, and all was good.

The next morning, I woke up, made coffee and quietly sat in Mom's recliner, mindlessly catching up on work email. I was preparing for an important conference call at 9 a.m.

Isabella came in to check on Mom about 7:30 a.m.

"All good, very peaceful night," I said.

Then I saw Isabella's face fill with panic as she took Mom's pulse.

"What's wrong?" I asked.

"She only has a few hours left, Sis."

I gave Isabella a quizzical look.

"It's her gurgling breathing," Isabella said. "Her

lungs are full of fluid."

Mom was drowning, just as she had feared.

I turned to look at Mom, lying on the bed. Her eyes were closed. Now that Isabella had pointed out the change in her breathing, I noticed it, too. Isabella was telling me how she had seen this so many times before in her patients, yet all I heard was today was the day she was leaving us. I left Isabella, who continued to talk nervously. I ran to call Augustine and Lena, our older siblings. We began the final countdown.

For the next hour, ten of us sat nervously at Mom's side, making small talk and telling stories of our childhood. I held Mom's forearm and gently stroked her forehead. She was getting more and more restless, and the sound of her wet, labored breathing was terrifying to hear.

Outside, it started to sprinkle. Gabriel and Joyce excused themselves to cover some of Mom's items left in the backyard. As I watched them dash between the raindrops, I thought how calm my 15-year-old son was, how strong he had been through this. I turned to look at Mom, and I thought about how much he adored her, too.

As the morning wore on, the conversation around Mom continued and she got more and more uncomfortable. I stood next to her, gently wiped her hair from her forehead and kissed her as I said, "Daddy planned a big barbecue for you, Mom, and everyone is there waiting to greet you. It started on Thursday and it's Friday, and you hate to be late. It's time for you to go, Mom. We will all be fine. I promise you — and I will always love you." To my surprise she calmed down and I sat next to her again, holding her arm.

Just then, Gabriel and Joyce broke in. "Did you see him?"

We gave them stunned looks. "See who?"

"A man, looking through the sliding glass door. On the patio," Gabriel said.

"What man?" Isabella asked.

"I didn't see his face, but he was wearing jeans, a plaid shirt and a cowboy hat," Gabriel said. "Joyce saw him, too."

She nodded. "When I called to him, he disappeared."

"What?" Isabella said. "He disapp --?"

I touched Isabella's arm. "I don't think she's breathing, Sis."

She jumped up from her chair, and we all surrounded Mom's bed. I was on her right side and Isabella on her left with everyone else around her, and we were all holding hands with tears welling up in our eyes. Joyce took out her stethoscope and listened to Mom's chest. My sister asked Joyce to call her time of death.

"10:28 a.m.," said Joyce.

With tears streaming down my cheeks, I gently took the oxygen nasal cannula off Mom's face.

"Daddy came for her," I said. "That's who was looking in the window. He came to take her home."

Isabella agreed. "Yes, he came for his Rosie."

Chapter Eleven

Farewell, With Love

There is nothing that prepares you for
the raw emotional pain

you will experience when you bid your
loved one farewell.

Have compassion for yourself

and your feelings.

It's most likely the greatest heartache
you will ever endure.

I'm sorry for your loss and sorrow.

Day 401, Friday, Jan. 20, 2012

Death had quietly come for our beloved mother as I held her arm and the rest of our family sat around her. As I looked down at her still, peaceful body, I silently said goodbye. I was struck by the silence of her empty corpse. It was the first death I'd ever witnessed, and it was truly remarkable to see how quickly life exits a shell.

Gabriel stood at the end of bed, staring at her with tears running down his face. I hugged him, but it was clear that he needed to experience this alone. I quietly stepped aside. "Thank you for being here with me," I said.

I called our hospice nurse and told her that Mom had died. It was heartbreaking to say those words out loud. She calmly gave me her condolences and said she was sending someone over in about ten minutes to take care of the death certificate and other required paperwork. I called the mortuary next. They were kind and gentle too, and said that it would take approximately 30 minutes to pick up Mom's remains.

The hospice nurse arrived right on time and

started the paperwork. The doorbell rang again just a few minutes after the nurse arrived and it was the Rabbi Jackie, Mom's hospice spiritual adviser. "I'm not supposed to be here. But I had to come," she said with tears in her eyes as she hugged me at Isabella's front door. We walked into the great room, where she saw my raw, grieving family saying goodbye to Mom. Isabella explained that only one hospice team member was supposed to be with us right now, and I felt so blessed that the rabbi was breaking the rules to be with us on the saddest day of our lives.

"Would you like to say a prayer?" asked the rabbi through her tears. "Yes, yes, yes," we all said. We gathered around Mom's hospital bed. I stood on her right side near her head, holding her arm, and Isabella was on the left directly across from me, doing the same. The rest of the family stood close to her bed with their hands on various parts of her body. The rabbi started the prayer and asked us if we wanted to each share a prayer as well. She instructed us to say "pass" if we didn't want to say anything out loud as we began our prayers counter-clockwise. The grandchildren, including Gabriel, all passed. Joyce and Isabella shared loving tributes to Mom. When it was my turn, my heart was racing, tears streaming down my face. I spoke. "Beautiful Mom, thank you for being the best mother ever, for always listening to me, for the countless hours of accompanying me on my long commutes to and from work for over 20 years, for always accepting and forgiving me. I am eternally grateful for your love, and I look forward to seeing you again. Enjoy your party today and seeing all your family. I love you."

More family and hospice team members arrived to say their goodbyes to Mom. As they entered I welcomed them but stayed near Mom's bed. I couldn't leave her side. The hospice team members all said the same thing as they hugged me: "I'm not supposed to be here, but I had to come."

I understood why — they loved her too. All five of them lovingly said goodbye to her. I overheard someone say, "She's still warm" as she touched her.

The mortuary attendants arrived with a stretcher. I spoke to them for a few minutes and they asked me to request that the family go outside. They said it was often very hard for families to witness the body being taken away. I quickly ushered the 30 or so family and friends to Isabella's patio. I returned with Mom's dog Gigi. "I'll be okay. I don't want to leave her alone while this happens," I said. I was holding Gigi in my arms as the attendants gently maneuvered Mom into a large black body bag. As the attendant zipped it closed, I stopped him before he closed it over Mom's face. I blessed her forehead one last time and kissed her. The attendant gently closed the zipper.

The attendants were speaking to me, but I had no idea what they were saying. Gigi and I followed the stretcher outside to the van, where they loaded Mom into the back. I wanted Gigi to see Mom leave. It seemed crazy, but I wanted her to know that Mom's scent was leaving the house and would never be returning.

After they drove away, I went to the patio and advised the family and hospice team that she was gone. They quietly returned to the great room.

I stayed out on the patio for a few minutes and called John. He offered to come to Santa Maria immediately, but I told him to hold off. I needed him at the service, but most likely I wouldn't know all the details for a few days.

Next, I called Jessie's dad and gave him the news. He was going to tell Jessie when he picked him up from school in a few hours. My heart hurt that I wouldn't be the one telling him — and more importantly, there to console him.

Back in the house, everyone sat in the great room talking about Mom. Isabella abruptly ran out of the room, and Joyce followed her. I looked at Mom's empty bed and knew that we had to get it out of the great room quickly. I removed the bedding and started washing everything. I called the hospital rental equipment company. They told me they could come in a few hours to pick up Mom's hospital bed, oxygen compressor, serving tray, etc.

More family arrived. My younger brother Peter had driven from Los Angeles, just missing seeing Mom by about 30 minutes. Our dear friends Sol and Emelio Gomez and one of their daughters from Mexico drove all night, missing her by an hour or so. It was a surreal experience to recount Mom's death as family and friends continued to arrive. By the time everyone had arrived, the house was brimming with about 50 people.

After about an hour, I went upstairs to check on Isabella. I saw her curled up in a fetal position on her bed, shattered with grief. "Can I bring you anything?" I asked.

"No, thank you," she said.

"We need to call everyone, Isabella. Do you want me to do it?" I looked at my sister.

"Oh, yes, can you please?" she said. "I just can't."

"Sure, Sis, no problem. I'll use Mom's phone book."

I left Peter, his wife and our dear friend Sol in charge of our guests as I escaped to my niece's bedroom to make the phone calls. First, I called Maria. She couldn't believe it. She was devastated, eventually having to pass the phone to her husband so I could give him the details of Mom's passing. The rest of the more than 60 calls were pretty much the same. The recipient of my call started crying immediately, shattered by the news and wanting every detail of her passing, which drove me to try to console them. By the end of the experience I was emotionally and physically exhausted.

I called St. Louis de Montfort Catholic Church and made an appointment for Saturday afternoon to meet with Father Manuel, who had been my high school teacher. Then I scheduled an appointment to meet with the mortuary the same day.

When I returned to the great room, Gabriel was making chicken sandwiches for everyone.

"Would you like one?"

"Yes, please," I replied, so proud of my son.

By 2 p.m. a polite young man from the rental company came to remove all of Mom's equipment. We completed the paperwork quickly, and in minutes, all of Mom's hospice items were gone.

I summoned Gabriel and the rest of the teenagers to help me restore Isabella's great room to its pre-Mom furniture arrangement. We began to clean the floors and move furniture. Behind the cushions where Mom's hospital bed had been, I found a notebook and a half-eaten box of See's candy. Mom's Christmas candy. It brought a smile to my face as I thought of her hiding her candy from all of us. Oh, how she loved her sweets. I put them away along with the notebook. But then I stopped and opened it to find an unfinished letter to my estranged brother Francis. *No matter what you've done, I will always love you…*

It felt wrong to continue to read it, so I put it away with the candy. Poor Mom, always trying to fix things and always forgiving everyone.

The teenagers were a big help, and we had the room back in shape in no time. It was my meager attempt to help Isabella. And although we had returned the dining room table to where Mom's hospital bed had been, I found myself looking for Mom's bed. I thanked the children for helping me, and they were very quiet. This was so unlike them.

I spoke to Jessie after he got out of school. He was quiet, and I knew he was upset about his grandmother. I longed to be with him, but I needed to stay in Santa Maria for a few more days. I hoped to return to Redwood City on Sunday.

I went upstairs to check on Isabella again. She was in the same position that I'd left in her hours before. I updated her on the church and mortuary appointments. "I can't go with you, Sis. I'm sorry," she said.

"No problem, Isabella. I got it. Lena offered to go with me. I'll take it from here and continue to update you so you know what's going on." Lena was our older half-sister, and I was so grateful that she'd offered to help me with Mom's services.

"Thank you." I noticed she was crying.

"No worries, Sis. You took such good care of her for so long that I'm happy to take this on and make sure Mom has the best send-off ever."

I felt I should fill her in, so I told her the rental company had come for the bed and we had put her furniture back in place. "I was trying to make it easier for all of us. I thought it would be too much for you to see her empty bed for a few days. I hope it's OK that I acted so quickly."

"Thank you. I'm going to look for it anyway, but it's probably better that they picked it up," Isabella said.

I waited for a few moments and decided to continue with what I feared might be a controversial conversation. We needed to make decisions about the funeral. "I think we should have a closed casket for Mom. I just don't want her body being poked and prodded. She suffered enough, and she's so thin. I don't want anyone gawking at her. What do you think?"

"The old timers always have an open casket, but I'm with you, Diana. I don't want her to be on display," she said. "But what do we tell everyone?"

"I think we tell them it was Mom's wish, and that will be fine. I also don't want the kids' last memory of their beloved grandma to be in a casket, barely recognizable. We'll find a great photo of her and place it next to the casket and make it all beautiful instead of morbid and scary," I said.

"It's a good idea, Sis, and if anyone is upset about not being able to see her body, I'm sending them your way," she said, half-smiling.

"Please do. I can handle that," I said.

"You know, that enchilada and lemon doughnut were the last things she ever ate." Isabella was crying again. "She stopped eating after Monday night. I knew we were so close, but I still can't believe she's gone, Diana."

"I can't either, Sis. And she's finally no longer suffering," I said, then I stopped myself. It was what I had been saying to everyone I called when they cried. I explained. "I didn't mean to try it on you, too. I'm sorry." I hugged her again, wishing that there was something I could say that would make her hurt less.

Our cousin Carlos was the first to arrive with food. He brought some chicken cacciatore with steamed rice for dinner about 6 p.m. Mom's nieces arrived a few minutes later with homemade brownies. By 8 p.m. we had a table full of desserts, casseroles, enchiladas and more. I was so grateful for all the delicious food. I didn't feel like cooking, and the house was full of hungry people. So many times I had delivered Mom's food to family members when they were grieving. Now I understood what a blessing that truly was.

About 9 p.m. I took a plate up to Isabella and tried to get her to eat a little. To my delight, she did.

"You should check out the dessert table," I said, and she finally agreed to come downstairs for a little while. Most of our extended family had left. I saw her look at the furniture. She thanked the kids sitting around the great room for helping me rearrange it. The TV quietly played in the background, and the kids were all immersed in their phones. Isabella took a look at the snack table and sampled a brownie. We chatted for a few minutes, and she returned to her room.

I slept upstairs, as there was no need to sleep downstairs in the great room anymore. Little Gigi slept with me. Poor Gigi sobbed all night. I had never heard her make sounds like that. She clearly knew that Mom was gone and she was grieving, too. It broke my heart.

First thing Saturday morning I woke up and went downstairs to make coffee. I was half asleep when I entered Isabella's great room, and I was shocked back into reality when I saw that Mom's hospital bed and oxygen compressor were gone. The silence was haunting, and my eyes filled with tears as I made coffee. Isabella was right. We would all be looking for Mom in this room for a long time to come.

At St. Louis de Montfort Catholic Church, Lena, met me in the parking lot. I was grateful to have her with me as we met with Father Manuel. "Your mother was such a wonderful woman," he began. "I remember her bringing us delicious Mexican food."

"My mother was an amazing cook," I said. "You were one of my favorite high school teachers and my mom's favorite priest."

He walked me through the funeral pamphlet, pointing out where we needed to select readings and other opportunities to personalize her Mass. To my delight, we were going to be able to include lots of friends and family in Mom's farewell Mass.

"Who's going to do her eulogy?" he asked.

"Diana," Lena said.

"That's what I thought," Father Manual replied with a proud smile.

Before leaving, we met briefly with his office manager and scheduled Mom's funeral for 11 a.m. Thursday.

I returned to a bustling house, loud and full of life. The Gomez family was visiting and had brought more food.

I told everyone when the funeral would be, pulled out the funeral book and started to explain my ideas about Mom's service. I asked the Gomez family to participate and asked their daughter, Clementina, if she could help select the readings. Clementina was one of Mom's godchildren and adored my mother. She was also a very active practicing Catholic, and I knew she'd do a great job selecting the Scriptures.

A few hours later, I left for my appointment with the florist. I was a longtime customer, and the owner was very kind. He offered to show me pictures of casket sprays. I explained that it wasn't necessary. I knew what I wanted. I had a long time to think about it. I placed the order and gave him the funeral details.

By the time I reached my parked car, I was openly sobbing. I got in the car and started driving. I drove for about 20 minutes and parked on the side of the road. I'd driven to our old address, the farm where I'd grown up, the same spot where a few months earlier I had kicked the dirt and screamed at God about losing Lulu. The sky was gray and it was windy. I cried as loud as I could. It was soothing to be here. And I just let the tears gush out. I stayed for about an hour.

Later that evening, I sent the musician a list of the songs Mom had selected for her funeral. I had made lots of progress on Mom's funeral service, and it felt good.

Now I needed to call the pallbearers. Mom had left a handwritten note listing some of the people she wanted. I found the first name on the list — Mom's nephew — and called him.

"I'm sorry, Mia, I don't think I can do it. I'm having trouble with my knee."

"No worries. I'm sorry to hear that. Take care," I said, and hung up.

I turned to Isabella. "Mom's list of pallbearers isn't going to work. They are too old. I think we need to upgrade the list. What about including some of Mom's grandchildren?"

"I love that idea," she said.

Immediately, Gabriel and Lucas, Joyce's teenage son, threw their names into the hat. Christina, Isabella's youngest daughter, volunteered, too.

"Do you think it's okay to have a girl pallbearer?" Isabella said.

"Father Manuel told me about a recent funeral where all the pallbearers were the woman's granddaughters," I said.

"Mom would have loved this, Diana."

Soon the lineup was complete. Mom's pallbearers were a combination of my older brother, her favorite nephew and grandchildren, including Jessie. It was a varied group with one thing in common: They adored Mom and knew her extremely well.

The following morning, I met with the mortuary. It was a short meeting. Mom and I had sorted out all the details before her death, and I had all the notes. I had to get the obituary to them the next day. We talked about the video I was making, her rosary and having a closed casket.

I was done with most of Mom's arrangements, and it was a huge relief. I went back to Isabella's to visit with family.

"Diana, didn't you call Adam's mom?" asked Isabella a few minutes after I arrived.

"She was one of first people I called. She didn't answer, and I left her a voicemail," I said, feeling a knot grow in my stomach. I'd never heard back from her and I completely forgot to call her again. I was consumed with funeral arrangements and grief. Adam was only nine years old and Mom's only great-grandson, and he adored her. I braced myself for what came next.

"He called a few minutes ago, and Lucas answered the phone. He wanted to come visit his great-grandma, and Lucas replied, 'She's dead, did you forget?' Adam started crying and had no idea she had died. His mom is driving him over right now."

Just as I'd feared. Poor Adam, what a terrible way for him to hear the news.

"I'll tell his mother when she gets here that you called her, but she's pretty upset with us," Isabella said.

"Blame it on me, Sis. I don't have time for any drama today. It's a shame that Adam found out like this, but all I can do is apologize." I felt annoyed.

About 15 minutes later, I greeted Adam's mother at the door. It took every ounce of self-control to apologize. I wanted to yell at her for even thinking that any of my family would do anything intentional to hurt Adam. It never mattered to Mom or any of us that she and my nephew were no longer together. Adam was family. I assured her that I had called her and there had been some freak accident of technology

that hadn't recorded my message. I even sh
my phone so she could see proof that I'd
the morning that Mom died. She calmed down before
leaving, and Adam stayed with us.

Gabriel and I drove home to Redwood City
later that afternoon. I was looking forward to seeing
John, Jessie and little Sophia. But as we started our
drive home, Gabriel said, "I wish you would have let
me stay with them."

Even as I explained we'd be back Tuesday
night to get ready for the memorial service and that he
needed to be back in school for a couple of days, I
knew what he would say.

"My grandma died, Mom. I don't feel like going
to school," Gabriel said. I felt his grief pierce me as he
looked away.

"You've already missed so many days, Gabriel.
And Grandma would never want you to get behind in
school because of her," I said compassionately.

He didn't reply and I knew he wasn't thrilled,
but I decided it was best to give him space. Clearly
we were headed toward a large argument if I kept on.

We were both grieving, and even the air in the car felt heavy with our sadness.

John and Sophia greeted us in the driveway, and it was so good to see them. I cried as John held me. I'd been trying to remain strong for the rest of my family for the last couple of days, and it was such a relief to have John's strong arms around me. Jessie had been staying with his father since Mom died.

Gabriel dashed inside and within a few minutes informed me that his dad was coming to get him, and he and Jessie were going to spend the night with his father. I was relieved. That gave me an evening to regroup. I knew I'd be in a better place the next day to help my grieving sons. John took me to a nice, quiet late dinner and listened to me go on and on with every detail of Mom's death and how surreal it felt to be planning her funeral. He reminded me that he was here for me and would help with absolutely anything.

As soon as we returned from dinner, I started working on the final draft of Mom's obituary, which I had to email to the mortuary that night. "May I read it to you? And can you please give me honest feedback?"

"Of course, Babe." He sat down next to me on our sofa and gently placed his arm around me.

Beloved Mother, Grandmother,
Aunt and Friend

Mrs. Rose Ybarra Silva died peacefully Jan. 20 after a long illness, surrounded by her family at her daughter's home. She was the beloved mother of Augustine Silva, Lena Silva, Matthew Silva, Eva Silva, Isabella Silva, Francis Silva, all from Santa Maria; Diana Silva, Redwood City; Peter Silva, Walnut; and Dominic Silva, Ventura. Numerous grandchildren, great-grandchildren, nieces, nephews, in-laws and friends will dearly miss her.

Mrs. Rose Silva was preceded in death by her husband, Joseph Peter Silva, and all of her six siblings (Nueves, Amelia, Maria, John, Henry, Angel).

Mrs. Rose Silva was born on October

26, 1927, in Betteravia, just outside of Santa Maria. She was a devoted mother, homemaker and remarkable cook. Her homemade tortillas, tamales, chili beans and cupcakes were legendary. She was cherished and dearly loved by all who knew her.

She was also a huge sports fan (49ers, SF Giants and Lakers). She could rival Google with all her sports knowledge. In her golden years, she loved to travel, and considered her visit to the Holy Land and Vatican her most cherished trip.

Rosary services for Mrs. Rose Silva will be held at Dudley Hoffman mortuary on Wednesday, January 25th @7:00PM and Funeral Mass at St. Louis De Montfort Church on Thursday, January 26th @11:00AM.

"It's perfect, honey," John said, hugging me and handing me a facial tissue to wipe the tears from my cheeks.

"Thank you, John. I know that some of my family will be upset that I've expanded the list of her children to include half siblings and two grandchildren. And while she gave birth to only three of us, I know that she considered all nine of us to be her children and I wanted to tell her truth."

"It's absolutely perfect," he said. "Leave the children in and send it now before you change your mind."

The next morning, I took Gabriel and Jessie to school. It was the first time I'd seen Jessie since Mom's death, and he was quiet. It was clear that he didn't want to talk about the upcoming funeral. After dropping them off, I picked up my phone, found Mom's number and before realizing that she would never be answering again, her picture came up on my screen. I stopped myself from hitting the call button. I had wanted to call her and ask about Jessie and Gabriel. How could I help them with their grief? My eyes welled up with tears.

I went to my saved voicemail and saw one message from Mom dated Jan. 5, 2012, two weeks before she died. I bravely listened. "Diana, love you. Just called to say good night, I'll talk to you tomorrow, love you." The tears gushed down my face as my new reality began to settle in. A world without my best friend.

Somehow I managed to pull myself together when I got home. The only thing I could do for Mom now was to give a beautiful, heartfelt send-off. The biggest task left was to create a memorial movie for her rosary. I was creating the story of her life in chronological order, and feeling so grateful that Jessie had scanned all of her photo albums. I went through the 1,200 photos and selected about 200 for the first draft. After reviewing all the photos, I realized that I needed more recent photos because hers ended about 20 years ago. I went to our den and pulled down a large box of pictures that I was hoping would have good photos of Mom and our family. When I opened the box, I found a perfectly wrapped, flat square-shaped jewelry box. To: Diana, Love, Mom.

My heart was racing as I opened up the box. Inside was a beautiful silver heart with shiny stones all over it, on a silver chain. It was gorgeous. Where did it come from? Did she slip it in years ago and I never saw it until now? My mind was racing as I took the glittering heart from its box and placed it around my neck.

Later I told John about the mystery gift. "Babe, it must have been in there for a long time, and she probably forgot to ask you about it," he said.

"I don't know, John. It's so weird that I found it today of all days when I'm creating her movie," I said.

"I can't believe it's a gift from the other side," John said.

I could see he was trying hard to convince me that there was a logical explanation. I didn't really care if my thoughts were illogical. I was so grateful to have this last beautiful gift from my sweet mama.

About midnight I finished her movie, feeling pleased with the 20-minute tribute that featured wonderful photos of Mom with her beloved family accompanied by beautiful music by Andrea Bocelli, Il Divo and Michael Bublé.

The last thing I did before going to sleep a few hours later was to make a CD of the music to be played in the mortuary before and after her rosary. It was a mix of Latin music, mariachi, ballads, Motown, R&B, Elvis Presley, Tom Jones and Engelbert Humperdinck songs, a great combination of her favorites.

Day 405, Tuesday, Jan. 24, 2012

We arrived Tuesday night to a quiet house. I could feel Isabella's sadness as she told me about the dress she had selected for Mom to wear in her coffin. Isabella recounted her memory of seeing Mom, happy and beautiful in the gorgeous black dress at an evening wedding, and now it was the last thing she'd ever wear. I hugged her as tears rolled down her face. Isabella had been taking care of Mom for 13 months, and I think she realized that picking her final outfit was truly the last thing she'd ever do for her.

"Do you want to see the video?" I said.

"Not tonight," she said.

Isabella's house was full of out-of-town guests, and we were staying at Maria's house about a mile away. I looked forward to the visit. Maria and Carlos welcomed us warmly into their home, and it was calm and quiet. I went to bed fairly early so I could work on Mom's eulogy. Gabriel and I were going to do it together. He'd go first, and I'd follow him. I finished most of the eulogy, but I wasn't happy with it. I was good with Gabriel's section, but mine didn't feel right.

The next morning, I got up early and went to Isabella's so she could see Mom's movie. I needed her to see it before I took it to the mortuary. She watched it first with her daughter, Christina while I waited in the other room, praying that she'd be okay with it because I didn't have a lot of time to make edits.

At last she called me in. "I love it, Diana," she said. "It's fantastic. Thank you. It must have taken you forever to make it."

"About 18 hours, but it's all good, as long as you really think it tells her story," I said.

"It's really good," Christina added.

I gave Gabriel his eulogy draft. "These are just

my suggestions, Gabriel. Please edit them, put them into your voice. But it's your job to explain Grandma's various gifts during the procession and you can do that any way you like. I was merely trying to help," I said.

"Thanks, Mom. I might need to change it a lot to sound like me," Gabriel said, glancing at the page.

"That's completely okay, Gabriel. Thank you for doing this for your grandma," I said as I hugged him. He'd stayed with his Aunt Isabella the night before, and he looked tired. I wondered how much he was able to sleep. I suspected that he was grieving much more than I knew or he cared to share.

Our friend Clementina had come by Isabella's when I was going over the eulogy draft with Gabriel, and as a high school literature teacher, she quickly jumped in and helped Gabriel translate the proposed eulogy into his words.

Family and friends had packed into Isabella's house. I took this opportunity to explain that I would be making one last visit to the mortuary around 1 p.m., and the mortuary had told me to bring anything we wanted to put in Mom's coffin: letters, teddy bears, blankets and so on. "Anything you want to include, please get it to me by 12:30."

Immediately Jessie started writing her a letter. It was about four pages front and back when he put it into an envelope and sealed it. The mementos flooded in — letters, a flower, a soft blanket and pictures. I put the treasures in a bag and went to the mortuary by myself.

When I arrived, a funeral attendant assured me he would take care of the items to be placed in Mom's coffin. Another attendant came to walk me to the viewing room. I almost fell over when I saw her rose-colored casket at the front of the room with the spray of pink baby roses laid over it. Her photo was propped up on an easel next to it. It looked so beautiful. There were several large sprays of other flowers, too.

"Is everything okay?" the attendant asked.

"Yes, it looks amazing. It's just a shock to actually see it." I struggled to hold back my tears. The kind gentleman gave me a tissue.

"Do you need us to move anything?" he asked.

"Not a thing," I said. "It's stunning."

The man walked to the front of the room and

flipped a switch. A giant projection screen dropped from the ceiling. A few moments later my mother's movie started playing. It looked amazing, and the sound was perfect.

Back at Isabella's, I picked up Jessie so we could get back to Maria's house and get ready for Mom's rosary.

"How does it look, Mia?" Sol Gomez said tenderly, sounding like an older loving sister instead of a dear family friend who had driven from Mexico.

I burst into tears. "I'm sorry, Sol, it looks so beautiful, but it was a shock to see it." And there I sat, openly crying in front of everyone in the room. Sol rushed to me and enveloped me in a hug. In one swift move, she ushered me to the hallway, discreetly out of sight of the rest of the group.

"Oh, Mia, one of us should have gone with you," Sol said. "You are so strong. I think we all forget that you are grieving too."

I felt her arms around me, and I was grateful. "I know that she is no longer suffering and in heaven, happy, with her mother, brothers, sisters, and my dad, but I miss her so much."

"I know, Mia, that's how I feel about my parents," she said.

Back at Maria's, I had to get ready for the rosary. The plan was for me to arrive at 4 p.m. to greet guests who arrived for the viewing. John and the boys would come around 6 p.m., and the rosary would start at 7 p.m.

"Are you sure you don't want me to go with you?" John asked as I gathered my purse and car keys.

"No, Babe, just get the boys there on time. Isabella will meet me there. I'll be okay." I walked toward my car, then I turned back. "And, thank you." I kissed him goodbye.

I walked into the mortuary exactly at 4 p.m., and Isabella wasn't there. She was always late, I thought. But how could she do this today? She promised she'd be on time. I needed her. After waiting for ten minutes, I left the viewing room and went to the hallway to call her and demand that she get down here immediately. As I pulled out my phone I heard Mom say, "Not today. Don't fight with your sister, Diana." I put the phone away.

Mom's first guest arrived 15 minutes earlier than the official viewing start time, but everything was ready and I did my best to be gracious, even though I felt so alone.

Thankfully my oldest half-sister, Eva, arrived about 4:30 p.m. to help. I hadn't seen her very much in the last few years, and I was beyond thrilled to have her there to help me. "Oh, Eva, thank you so much for coming so early to help greet Mom's guests," I said as I gave her a big hug. "I wanted to help you with this, Diana," she said. I knew instinctively that she knew Isabella would be late today like she always was, and that's why she'd come so early, but neither of us brought it up. Eva had our father's gift of gab, and was gracious and kind to everyone as they arrived. She was the perfect co-host.

As expected, Mom drew a big crowd of family and friends who arrived early for the viewing. John came early with the boys, about 5:30 p.m.

"I knew she was going to be late," John said, annoyed, as he looked around for Isabella.

"It is what it is, Babe," I said. "Eva has been a

godsend, and I'm fine."

Isabella and her family arrived a few minutes before everything started, and she had some major excuse for being so late. I didn't make a big deal about her tardiness. I was no longer angry at her.

By the time Father Manuel arrived, the room was bustling with guests.

"What a great turnout," Father Manuel said as he gathered all of us who were going to do the readings.

"We have a huge family, and she was so loved," I said.

Just then, the screen dropped, the movie began to play and everyone watched it quietly.

When the rosary ended, the guests formed an orderly line, walked to the front of the room and knelt at Mom's casket, and then came by each row filled with immediate family, daughters, half-children and grandchildren, and gave us their condolences. It was an endless parade of hugs and hearing how special our mother was. There were also lots of comments about Mom's movie and how much they loved it. They were shocked that it included a photo of my Mom when she was only five years old with my grandmother and all her older sisters, a photo no one had ever seen. And they especially loved one of the last photos with Mom smiling while she held Marisol.

Back at Isabella's, I reminded all the pallbearers that they had to be on time for Mom's funeral tomorrow. In the kitchen, Peter was busy marinating chicken and prepping for Mom's giant reception. The kitchen smelled like garlic and onions as he expertly cut whole chickens in half and placed them in the marinade. I could see Mom instructing him on how to make the marinade, cut the chicken, etc. She had been a great teacher, and I was grateful that my brother had learned how to make some of her amazing food, too.

"What are you going to cook tomorrow?" Gabriel asked me before we left.

"Nothing," I said, feeling grateful for others volunteering to take care of all the food. I knew that I would continue to cook her recipes, but not today. I feared that stepping into the kitchen without her would consume me with grief and loss, and possibly shut me down. "I have too much to do for the funeral, and it's okay. We have lots of amazing cooks in our family." I was thankful that Mom had taught several of us how to cook. We would keep her memory alive by continuing her legacy of cooking her amazing recipes and enjoying them together. She really had no understanding of how much she'd taught us about food and life. "Peter is organizing the barbecue crew, Patty is bringing beans from Jocko's restaurant and others are bringing desserts, salsa and salads and Spanish rice."

I could tell Gabriel was shocked by my response, but I was really trying to let everyone help instead of taking everything over like I normally did. Mom was beloved, and I was doing my best to let everyone who wanted to help with her reception and farewell participate. I needed their help.

Maria and Carlos were watching TV when we arrived at their house. "Your mom sure had a lot of people tonight," Maria said. "And there will be more tomorrow, Mia."

"Many of my dad's relatives I hadn't seen for

years," I added.

It had really felt nice to see so many people — neighbors, family, friends.

"Her movie was fantastic, Diana. Will you make me a copy of it?" Maria said.

"Of course, and I'll give you a copy of all her pictures. Jessie scanned all of her photo albums, and I'm going to burn CDs with all the photos for anyone who wants them."

"That was a really good idea, Diana."

"I didn't want anyone to fight over her pictures."

John checked in with me later about whether I was ready. He offered to review the eulogy.

"I finished it, but I don't like it," I said. "It's too flowery and light, and doesn't capture the essence of Mom's contribution to my life and to her family. I'm not happy with it at all."

"Can you rewrite it?" John said.

"I want to go in a completely different direction," I said. "It's very controversial, and I'm not sure how everyone will take it."

"Is it the truth? Would your Mom approve?"

Yes, those were the right questions. "I think she would love it."

"Then you know what you have to do," he said. "Are you going to rewrite it now?"

"I don't need too. It's right here." I touched my heart.

When we arrived at the church the next morning, I was delighted to see all of our pallbearers there on time. I thanked them. I had one more detail to adjust. I spoke to Father Manuel to explain that Gabriel would accompany me with the eulogy. He agreed to it, but I could tell he was concerned because Gabriel was only 15.

"Actually," I said, reading his thoughts, "you need to be more concerned about me than Gabriel."

Gabriel had been performing on stage for eight years and was an accomplished singer. His years on stage had also made him a remarkable public speaker. I knew he was going to do an amazing job delivering his piece of Mom's eulogy.

The hearse arrived, and I watched as attendants moved Mom's coffin to the back of the church in the accompanying hallway. The mortuary attendants lined up the pallbearers around Mom's casket and instructed them how to take her to the front of the church. I felt so proud of Mom's grandkids. They all looked great in their dark suits and ties, and Christina looked fantastic in her black dress. They were serious and respectful. As I looked at them I knew Mom was proud, too. Several guests had gathered in the back of the church to accompany Mom on the procession into the church. I noticed many of them were already crying.

The music started, and it was time.

Father Manuel joined us in the back of the church and blessed the coffin with holy water and incense. There was a small ceremony and prayer with a white cloth that was spread over Mom's casket. The procession started, and we followed the casket into the church with beautiful music playing. The female singer sounded like a young Linda Ronstadt as she played guitar and a pianist accompanied her. Isabella and I walked next to Father Manuel, and we sat directly behind Mom's casket and pallbearers, with our families behind us. The church was packed with sober-looking guests in dark clothing. There were easily at least 200 people. Mom's picture was on the altar next to her casket.

The funeral proceeded flawlessly, and before I knew it Father Manuel signaled Gabriel and me to come to the altar. Time for her eulogy. Gabriel went first and did an amazing job talking about his grandmother's gifts and passions. Several family members brought my mother's tortilla rolling pin, *molcajete*, Lakers jersey, Giants cap and picture with Pope Paul II to the front of the church near Mom's casket. They placed the items on the table with Mom's picture. Near the end of Gabriel's eulogy, Renee brought up little Marisol and gave her to Father Manuel. He held Marisol for a moment and spoke about Mom's great-granddaughter, then returned her to Renee. Gabriel finished his section, and just as I'd predicted he did a wonderful job. I was so proud of him.

Gabriel stepped away from the microphone, and I nervously stepped forward without any notes. "First of all, thank you so much for joining us today. It means so much to us to have you here with us. And as Gabriel shared, my mother, Rose, was a great cook and homemaker, a loving mother, sister, wife, grandmother and friend. ..."

Isabella and I had had a lot of time to think about Mom's greatest gift to us. We agreed it was her wisdom. Here is how I told the story of my mother's life:

"My mother, Rose, grew up in Betteravia, a small community for migrant farm workers about seven miles west of Santa Maria in a time when there was open segregation. She was a young woman in the early '40s, long before the civil rights movement and Dr. Martin Luther King. She was classified as a non-white whenever she left her small but safe community. This included going to school, going to Santa Maria or anywhere else. Her daily routine meant rides in the back of the bus, drinking from separate water fountains and going to the movies on designated nights reserved for non-whites.

"And although she endured these racial prejudices, she never told my sister and me anything about them when we were growing up. She talked about her childhood in Betteravia, hard work, good food and family history, but not one single word about the racial prejudice she had personally endured.

"I was in college when I discovered my mother had endured racial discrimination similar to African Americans. We were learning about the civil rights movement, and I read somewhere about Santa Maria and its separate water fountains for non-whites. When I asked my mother about it, she confirmed that yes, she had been forced to use separate water fountains, ride in the back of the bus, only attend special movie nights and so much more. I was shocked and deeply saddened to learn that my sweet dear mother had been mistreated. I asked her why she had never told us about what had happened to her, about all the prejudice she had endured, and she said, "I wanted the hate to end with me. I didn't want you girls growing up to hate anyone because of the color of their skin and the way I had been wronged." She repeated again to emphasize:

"The hate ends with me."

"I was stunned when I heard her response and started to tell her that I could have separated her personal experiences from my own, but I stopped myself. I knew she was right; knowing that she had been the subject of racial discrimination would have changed my heart. With her wisdom, courage and foresight she gave us the gift to see people and not color. We are grateful for her love and wisdom, and we will miss her so much."

With that, I exited the altar.

As I walked back to my seat, I glanced at the guests. Everyone had tears rolling down their faces; there were no dry eyes. I returned to my seat, trembling, and shed my first tear. Mom had helped me hold it together and deliver her eulogy with no notes and directly from my heart. John and Isabella rushed to hug me.

"She's so proud of you," Isabella said. "That was so beautiful, Diana. Thank you. I could have never done that."

At the end of the funeral, I went up one last time to invite everyone to her reception. "Help us celebrate our mother's remarkable life."

In the car with John, we joined the funeral procession to the cemetery.

"So many people stopped me and said that this was the most beautiful funeral they had ever been to," I said as I wiped the tears off my face.

"It *was* beautiful, Babe," John said.

At the cemetery, we walked up to the hearse, following as the pallbearers carried Mom's coffin to her gravesite. The ceremony was brief. Amid the hugs and stories of how special my mother was, I was brimming with grief. But as everyone else turned to depart, I walked over to Mom's coffin and blessed and kissed it one last time.

Arriving at the reception hall, my first sensation was the smell of food. The oak wood barbecue, grilled chicken, French bread, chili beans, Spanish rice, salsa and salads smelled delicious and familiar. This was the preferred menu for all of Mom's big parties like baptisms, graduations, baby showers and Mother's Day. Mom would have approved of the chili beans because next to her own, Jocko's restaurant's were her favorite. She most likely would have re-buttered the French bread, because no one ever put enough butter on the bread. Peter, his family and crew had done an outstanding job preparing and cooking all the food. Mom would have absolutely loved it.

Everyone at the reception was complimentary of Mom's services and the wonderful food. They repeatedly told Isabella and me to please reach out if we needed anything. The outpouring of love and support from our family and friends was comforting. And it confirmed what I already knew: Mom was beloved by so many.

After lunch, while I was washing dishes with Isabella, she told me the unfortunate tale of Mom's desserts. "You're not going to believe it, Sis, they took all of the desserts. The back table had been full of brownies, cookies, pies and cupcakes. Now it was empty. I had been looking forward to that table all day, and now it's empty." She sounded defeated.

"It's Mom's karma, Isabella." I smiled for the first time that day. "She always took a plate or napkins full of treats from funerals, parties, etc. Don't you remember? I can't even tell you how many times I saw her pull out the carefully wrapped plate of dessert treasures from her purse with the excuse that she needed a little something for her evening milk or morning coffee. And we both sampled plenty of those stolen treasures with her. It's perfect that her goodies were all taken from her funeral. I love it."

Isabella smiled too. "When you look it that way, then yes, this is her doing," she said. "But I still want some brownies."

"I'll buy you some," I said, and we hugged each other.

***

On the way home on Highway 101, north, John drove as I stared out the window. Although familiar, today the green rolling hills and oak trees framed by the blue sky seemed entirely in a new light. My life would never be the same. But I absolutely knew how to keep her memory alive forever. I finally understood what made her cooking so remarkable. Mom added love to all of her recipes, and it had the power to transform an ordinary recipe into magic. And although

I'd never cook with her again, I could add my love to all of her amazing recipes.

Her last 13 months had also inspired me to want to live as she had.

I would listen to understand, love to share my heart — and be content with every moment of my life.

And then I added, "Hello, beautiful. I know you're listening, sweet Mama. When I come home, can you please greet me with a large plate of warm flour tortillas and some homemade butter. I love you!"

* * *

"We're all just walking each other home."
~Ram Dass

THE END

Our Family Recipes

Chicken Mole Rojo

This was one of my mother's favorites recipes. It can be challenging to make this complex sauce, but it's so worth it.

The thing to remember when practicing traditional recipes like this is to have fun and don't be afraid to spill a little sauce on your stove! It's all about the learning process and the memories.

For complete instructions go to:
https://www.youtube.com/watch?v=FZXXrUv-sTM&t=2s

NOTE: When I say head of garlic, I mean the whole thing, not just one clove!

Important tools

Molcajete to crush your garlic

Food processor

Cast iron skillet

Ingredients

3 lbs. boneless skinless chicken breasts

2 heads of garlic, crushed, divided

2 medium yellow onions, chopped, divided

6 each Pasilla, Nuevo Mexico, California and Guajillo dried chiles

¾ cup flour

¾ cup olive oil

½ teaspoon cloves

Salt to taste

Directions

Step One: Boil chicken breasts

1. Add chicken, 1 head peeled crushed garlic, 1 finely chopped onion, 12 cups water, salt to taste.

2. Cook for about 45 minutes until completely cooked.
3. Remove chicken breasts, cool and shred into medium-sized pieces.
4. Save chicken broth.

Step Two: Rehydrate chiles to create chile nectar

1. Add chiles, the second cup of finely chopped onion, and crushed garlic into a pan, with 8 cups of water and simmer for about 30 minutes (until chiles are soft)
2. Remove chiles from water and remove stems. Place in food processor with onions, garlic and broth. Puree.
3. Pour mixture through fine strainer to remove seeds. The mixture may be very thick and require more chile broth to work through strainer.

Step Three: Prepare Roux

1. Pour oil into cast iron skillet and heat.
2. Test heat of oil with a wooden spoon. Once it bubbles around wooden spoon, add flour and constantly mix to keep from burning.
3. Once flour is a deep brown, pour about 1 cup of chile nectar and 8 cups of chicken broth into mixture. Turn down heat and whisk to remove lumps. High heat will result in the mole bubbling excessively. May need more broth to get desired consistency.
4. Add cloves, salt and chicken. Simmer for at least 30 minutes.
5. Serve warm. Great with orange rice and flour tortillas. Enjoy!

Chili Beans

This is my mom's legendary recipe, and a family favorite. They are great for barbecues, served with toasted garlic bread, in burritos or chimichangas or plain in a large bowl with some cheese and guacamole. Enjoy!

NOTE: When I say head of garlic, I mean the whole thing, not just one clove!

Ingredients

2 lbs. of dried pinto beans

20 cups of water

1 lb. of lean ground beef

1 lb. of bacon (best to use unflavored)

1 lb. of chorizo

2 large onions, chopped

1 large sweet red pepper, chopped

1 medium head of garlic, crushed

3 tablespoons dried California chile powder

½ teaspoon cumin

Salt and pepper to taste

Directions

Step One: Cook beans

1. Add beans, water and salt to a large stock pan and boil for about 4 hours. Can also soak overnight and shorten the cooking time to about 2 hours.
2. Beans are done when they are soft and tender.

Step Two: Cook the following items

1. Fry ground beef and drain excess fat.
2. Dice bacon into small pieces, fry until golden brown and drain excess fat.
3. Fry chorizo and cook for about 25 minutes.
4. Add finely chopped onions, red pepper and garlic to cooked chorizo and cook for another 10 minutes.
5. Add cooked ground beef, bacon and chorizo items to beans and mix well.
6. Add California chile powder, cumin, salt, and pepper to taste and simmer for 1-3 hours. To turn up the heat, add more chile powder.

Chocolate Cupcake Recipe

Ok, chocolate lovers here's the best cupcake recipe ever! Dark chocolate, cream cheese and chocolate chips; – it's seriously a chocolate/cheese lovers' dream come true. But be careful, they mysteriously disappear as soon as they come out of the oven.

Don't use reduced fat, low-sodium ingredients; they won't work. I usually encourage you to be creative with your cooking, but this is one time that you need to follow this recipe exactly, and you will be oh-so-thrilled with the results. If you decide to eat them warm, pairing them with a scoop of vanilla bean ice cream is a mind-blowing experience. If any of your cupcakes go uneaten for more than 24 hours, please refrigerate them. Enjoy!

Ingredients

1 devil's food cake mix + all ingredients on the back of box (eggs, oil, water)
Cream Cheese Filling

- 1 egg

- 2 eight-ounce Philadelphia cream cheese bars (don't substitute w/low fat, etc.)
- 12 ounces Toll House chocolate chips
- 1/2 cup of white granulated sugar
- 1 teaspoon vanilla

Directions

Step One: Prepare cupcakes

1. Line cupcake pans with paper or foil holders.
2. Preheat oven to 325 degrees.

Step Two:

Prepare chocolate cake mix (Bowl 1)

1. Mix cake mix and all ingredients per directions on the box.

Step Three:

Prepare cream cheese filling (Bowl 2)

1. Mix cream cheese, egg, sugar and vanilla with electric mixer until smooth and creamy.
2. Add in chocolate chips and mix well.

Step Four: Fill cupcakes

1. Fill each cupcake liner half full with chocolate cake mix (Bowl #1)
2. Add one large tablespoon to the top of each cupcake with the cream cheese filling (Bowl #2).

Step Five: Bake the cupcakes

1. Bake for 22 minutes and remove from oven.
2. Recipe makes approximately 24 – 30 cupcakes.

Crunchy Beef Tacos

My mama's crunchy tacos make me smile. Every bite is a treasure of delightful flavors wrapped in homemade corn taco shell goodness. Whether you stuff them with beef or fill them with veggies – or both – homemade crunchy taco shells are a flavorful way to step up the culinary quality of your dinner. They are easy to make, easy to customize, easy to love. Impress your family and friends with homemade crunchy beef tacos that taste like heaven!

For complete directions go to:

https://www.youtube.com/watch?v=6yWU-nxmKf4&t=39s

Ingredients

3 lbs. lean ground beef

1 cup salsa

Salt and pepper to taste

2 lbs. shredded cheddar cheese

3 finely chopped tomatoes

1 finely chopped iceberg lettuce

4 finely chopped serrano chiles

1 bunch of finely chopped cilantro

1 finely chopped yellow onion

2 chopped avocados

2 limes

1 point of sour cream or Mexican crema

2 cups Mazola corn oil

30 Guerrero corn tortillas (King size) at room temperature

Directions

Step One: Prepare taco fillings

1. Fry hamburger in large skillet and cook until well done.
2. Drain extra fat and return hamburger to the skillet.
3. Add salsa and simmer for 15 minutes.
4. Place all chopped veggies in serving bowls and top with a little fresh lime juice to keep fresh.

Step Two: Make homemade taco shells

1. In large frying pan, add oil and heat (oil is ready when it bubbles around a wooden spoon).
2. Place tortillas in hot oil and fry by submerging half of the tortilla in the oil for a moment and folding.
3. Turn over and fry other side.
4. Remove from oil and place in casserole dish with parchment paper.

Step Three: Assemble tacos

1. Fill with ground beef (about 2 tablespoons).
2. Top with fillings (your guests can build their own).
3. As soon as I've made 4 tacos, I let my guests start building their tacos while I continue to make more.

4. Nice to have salsa as a topping, too, and great to serve with Peruvian beans and orange rice. Enjoy!

Guacamole (Real)

So according to my mother, Rose, there is only one authentic guacamole recipe – hers, which she always referred to as the real one. Now my mother never shared how she became the official real guacamole recipe guardian, but as her oldest daughter with somewhat of a lifetime guacamole addiction, I never questioned her. I'm sure you have some of these recipe guardians in your families and understand how we must accept it as truth.

For complete instructions go to:

https://www.youtube.com/watch?v=7eqhjsx8lVs

Ingredients

5 large avocados

1 medium ripe tomato

¼ yellow onion

2 limes

½ bunch fresh cilantro

1 jalapeño chile (seeded)

3 serrano chiles (seeded)

Salt to taste

Directions

1. Finely chop tomato, onion, cilantro, chiles and place in bowl.
2. In separate bowl, add peeled avocados, lime juice, salt and mash together until chunky/creamy.
3. Combine chopped ingredients and avocados and mix well.
4. Serve immediately or refrigerate.
5. Can be refrigerated for up to 5 hours before serving. When preparing to refrigerate, cover with plastic wrap and squeeze all the air out. This will help preserve it and keep it from turning black.
6. Our guacamole can be eaten with chips, carne asada on tacos, in burritos and on chili beans and so much more...

Nine Pepper Chicken Soup

You might be thinking that nine peppers seem a little excessive, but I wouldn't recommend messing with a winning remedy. My mother told amazing stories of defeating the common cold with our family's chicken soup. And to the best of my knowledge my mother's accounts of our family's chicken soup's heroism against the common cold were all true.

This soup has some serious kick — three different types of peppers, onions, garlic, chicken, celery, fresh lime juice, tomatoes, zucchini, carrots, rice, cilantro and avocados. You can skip the chiles altogether if you don't want the heat and it's still yummy!

For complete instructions go to:https://www.youtube.com/watch?v=rDr7Zzu9hUc

Ingredients

2 lbs. boneless, skinless chicken, cubed

1 large yellow onion, finely chopped

6 – 8 cloves fresh garlic, crushed

6 stalks of celery, finely chopped

4 jalapeños peppers, finely chopped

4 serrano peppers, finely chopped

1 pasilla pepper, finely chopped

1 eight ounce can of tomato sauce

3 large carrots, chopped

3 zucchini, chopped

9 cups of water

2 Knorr chicken cubes

½ cup long grain rice

Salt and pepper to taste

2 limes

1 bunch of cilantro, finely chopped

1 – 2 avocados, chopped

Directions

1. Sauté chicken, onions, garlic, celery, 9 peppers for about 25 minutes.

2. Add tomato sauce, Knorr chicken cubes, salt, pepper, water and bring to a boil.

3. Turn heat down and simmer. Add rice, carrots, zucchini and lime juice and cook for another 25 minutes until rice is tender.

4. Serve in a bowl and garnish with cilantro and avocados.

Peruvian Refried Beans

This is my Tia Juvi's recipe, and my mother loved them. The secret to any refried beans recipe is the BACON. They are yummy in burritos, with grilled meats, enchiladas, in nachos and with orange rice.

For complete instructions go to:
https://www.youtube.com/watch?v=X0ILKZyIGnU

Ingredients

2 lbs. of dried, cleaned Peruvian beans

20 cups of water

Salt to taste (best to go light on salt, because the bacon will add more salt to their flavor)

1 lb. diced bacon

2 serrano chiles

Pepper

1 teaspoon onion flakes

Directions

Step One: Cook beans

1. Place beans in large stock/soup pot with water and salt and soak overnight.
2. Heat pot, and once boiling, lower heat to medium (low boil) and cook for about 2 hours until beans are tender.
3. Alternatively, don't soak and cook same as above for about 4 hours.

Step Two: Prepare beans and seasonings

1. Fry bacon in large frying pan/skillet until golden brown.
2. When bacon is about 75 percent done, place 2 whole serrano chiles in the frying pan.
3. Place cooked beans into frying pan with bacon and bacon fat. Simmer.
4. As beans simmer, begin to smash with potato smasher until creamy.

5. Add onion flakes, salt and pepper to taste.

Spanish Rice (Orange Rice)

Spanish Rice – or "Grandma's Orange Rice" – is simple to make and delicious with tacos, Mole Rojo, in burritos – you name it! The fragrance from this dish reminds me of my mama like no other! Enjoy!

For complete instructions go to:

https://www.youtube.com/watch?v=9LTvpG0YQJo

Ingredients

2 cups long grain white rice (rinse in strainer until water runs clear)

1 small can of tomato sauce

1/2 cup olive oil

1/2 yellow onion, finely chopped

2 jalapeño or serrano chiles

4-6 large garlic cloves, crushed

2 tablespoons of chicken Knorr broth

1/2 teaspoon cloves

Salt and pepper to taste

8 cups water

Directions

1. Heat oil in frying pan. Add washed rice and brown.

2. Once rice is dark brown, add in onions and chiles for about 2 minutes.

3. Mix crushed garlic, tomato sauce, chicken Knorr, cloves, salt and pepper and 8 cups of water in bowl.

4. Add items from bowl into the frying pan with rice. Bring to a boil. Reduce heat and simmer for about 30 minutes until rice is tender

Papas & Chorizo Chimichangas

Chorizo con papas (spicy pork sausage with potatoes) are one of my all-time favorite recipes. My mother made us chorizo con papas regularly, and on special occasions, she'd go the extra mile and make them into mouth-watering chimichangas. What makes chimichangas so special? Stuff chorizo con papas and cheddar cheese into a flour tortilla and fry it until golden brown – that's what.

Chimichangas are versatile and are great for lunch and make a great appetizer for dinner parties. But be careful! They are quite filling and addictive. If you're fortunate to have any left over, they will reheat nicely in a toaster oven.

Chorizo is sold in most supermarkets, but the best chorizo can be found in little Latin markets from the meat counter. And if available, the very best option is chorizo suelto (which means loose or in this instance, no sausage casing).

For complete directions go to:

https://www.youtube.com/watch?v=k9y3_7GFCp4

Ingredients

5 lbs. peeled, cubed russet potatoes

2 lbs. chorizo (suelto is the best)

1 cup water

Salt and pepper to taste

Optional Spices (Heat it up)

1 tablespoon chipotle powder

1 tablespoon California chile powder

1 teaspoon granulated garlic

1 teaspoon onion flakes

30 Guerrero flour tortillas (room temperature)

Directions

Step One: Cook chorizo and papas

1. Fry chorizo in large frying pan until fully cooked.
2. Add cubed potatoes, water and optional spices and cover.

3. Mix frequently and cook for 45 minutes, until potatoes are tender and fully cooked.

Step Two: Prepare chimichangas

1. Lightly brush edges of tortilla with oil.
2. Add ¼ cup of chorizo and papas to the center of the tortilla with a large spoon.
3. Fold 2 sides and fold again to create a rectangle.
4. Place on plate.

Step Three: Fry chimichangas

1. Heat oil in large frying pan (oil is ready for frying when oil bubble around wooden spoon).
2. Place chimichanga in hot oil with folded side down.
3. Flip once when golden brown, and brown second side.
4. Remove and place in serving dish lined with parchment paper.

5. A delicious option is to serve with guacamole and sour cream

Salsa Fresca

Nothing turns ordinary tacos, burritos, beans, grilled chicken, steak, pork, fish, eggs, soups or tortilla chips into a magical culinary experience as a little salsa fresca. Finely chopped peppers, cilantro, tomatoes, onions and lime juice come together and create a bold, delicious combination! It's a garnish with attitude, and no one can ever have just one serving, so make extra. And be warned, once you make this recipe, your family and friends will be requesting it often.

Oh and trust me you will never buy Picante that comes in a jar again. Or should I say your family and friends might not let you. But not to worry, it's easy, fast and yummy!

Ingredients

5 large tomatoes

½ medium onion

2 serrano peppers

2 jalapeño peppers

1/2 bunch of cilantro

2 limes

Salt to taste

Directions

Step One: Rinse all ingredients

1. Rinse and drain excess water from all ingredients.

Step Two: Chop all ingredients

1. Chop tomatoes, onion, peppers and cilantro super fine.
2. Best to remove most of the seeds from the peppers to keep down the heat.

3. Mix in a bowl.

Step Three: Add a final flourish

1. Add lime juice and salt. Mix well.
2. Eat immediately or keep in the refrigerator for up to 5 days.

Sonora Beef Enchiladas

I'm convinced that there is no greater combination of cheese, beef, spicy sauce and flour tortillas then our Sonora beef enchiladas. I made thousands of these with my mother for parties and fundraisers. It's a great recipe to make with someone. They embody Mexican comfort food, and orange rice is a delicious side dish. If you decide to freeze them, don't bake them before freezing.

Ingredients

3 lbs. lean ground beef
1 large onion, finely chopped
8 cloves of fresh garlic, crushed

Salt and pepper to taste

1 cup warm water

1 lb. grated Monterey jack cheese

1 lb. grated mild cheddar cheese

1 - 32 oz. can of mild Las Palmas sauce

1 cup of Mazola corn oil

30 Guerrero flour tortillas (room temperature)

Directions

Step One: Cook hamburger

1. Cook hamburger in a large frying pan and drain excess fat.
2. Add crushed garlic, onions, salt, pepper and 1 cup of water.
3. Simmer for 20 minutes until onion is tender.

Step Two: Prepare your enchilada assembly line

1. Place following items next to each other on your counter, work area:

- Cookie sheet needs to be in the center.
- Pour Las Palmas sauce in large bowl.

- Pour hamburger into a large bowl.
- Combine cheeses in large bowl.
- Place casserole dishes at the end of assembly line.

Step Three: Assemble enchiladas

1. Heat oil in large frying pan (oil is ready frying when oil bubbles around a wooden spoon).
2. With Tong #1, fry one tortilla in the hot oil. Flip once so it is fried briefly on both sides. Place on #1 cookie sheet.
3. With Tong #2, dip tortilla in Las Palmas sauce.
4. Remove from sauce and place on #2 cookie sheet.
5. Place about ⅓ cup of hamburger in the tortilla with a large spoon. Add about ¼ shredded cheese. Roll and place in casserole dish.
6. Once the casserole dish is full, cover with cheese and cover with tin foil.

7. Bake at 350 degrees for 30 minutes.

Acknowledgements

Thank you feels like an inadequate expression of my heartfelt gratitude for the super humans who helped me write, edit and publish my book. Every time I needed encouragement, support or a nudge, these delightful souls gave me a piece of their hearts and kept me going. Muchas gracias, blessings, love and light to my marvelous dream team!

Sean Head, my rock, and champion! You held my hand, wiped my tears and dared me to dream big.

Carolyn Flynn, my brilliant editor and soul sister! You helped me find my voice, kept me going and carried me over the finish line.

Kelly McClain and Lorraine Dahlinger, who designed my beautiful book cover. It makes my heart smile!

Julie Ashby, Melisa Caprio, Jenny Diebold, Terri La Mallorquina, Elizabeth Lindsay, Carmen Lopez, Jennifer Parker, Jackie Puerta and Eva Zermeño! My sisters, my loves, you lifted me up and believed in me!

Sophia, my devoted furry companion. You snuggled and kissed me just when I needed your love the most.

Our remarkable Beta Readers Group; Peg Fielder, Beth Ann Filippi, Terri Hanson Mead, Rosa Rajkovic and Jeanne Rosner, M.D. Your insights and recommendations were invaluable!

My family, friends and hospice volunteers who cared for, loved and cherished my beautiful mother until her last breath.

About The Author

Diana Silva is a San Francisco-based home chef, video blogger and radio host. Her Molé Mama Recipes YouTube channel celebrates family recipes, cooking delicious meals at home and adding love to every recipe. Diving into her Latina roots, she uses her magical molcajete, and other tools and techniques that make her food taste like grandma used to make back in Mexico. Along with her guest chefs, Diana explores recipes and traditions from all over the world and the stories that keep them alive.

Diana is calling everyone to return to their kitchens and to preserve their living and passed ancestor's favorite recipes and stories for future generations. "We need to try to preserve our cultures and not just let those favorite recipes disappear forever. The common thread of every cherished family recipe is that they were homemade with love, and that's the real secret ingredient," says Diana. For many home chefs, cooking is their preferred love language, and that's why we cherish their recipes.

Their love has the power to transcend an ordinary recipe into magic!

Diana encourages everyone to preserve those precious recipes and the stories that make them special. She invites those whose recipes have been lost or have faded over time to subscribe to her YouTube channel, there are plenty of recipes and traditions to share, and you just might be inspired to create your own because, "Every Recipe Tells a Story." Many of the recipes in this book are on her YouTube channel.

Diana credits her sweet mother Rose for her love of food, cooking and entertaining. She was just nine years old and when her culinary training began. Rose was making her legendary flour tortillas, and Diana's big job was to mix the masa. Rose expertly poured water, flour, salt and a little baking powder in the bowl and Diana eagerly put her small hands in the bowl and tried to follow her mother's patient instructions on how to mix it. Diana loved the way the sticky dough felt in her little fingers. She was so very proud and excited to help her mama.

Diana didn't understand the road she had embarked on that afternoon and the joy she'd experience cooking with her mother for more than 20 years. She is grateful for these treasured memories now that her mother is in heaven.

To watch Diana's cooking videos and learn more go to:

youtube.com/c/molemamarecipes.com

Molemama.com

facebook.com/molemama

@mole_mama

Disclaimer

The conversations in the book all come from the author's recollections, though they are not written to represent word-for-word transcripts. Rather, the author has retold them in a way that evokes the feeling and meaning what was said and in all instances, the essence of the dialogue is accurate. Most of the names have been changed to protect the privacy of Rose's family and friends.

70001686R00274

Made in the USA
Columbia, SC
01 May 2017